GOSPEL EDUCATION

GOSPEL EDUCATION

JESUS AS LORD OF THE CLASSICAL CHRISTIAN SCHOOL

NATE WALKER

BakerBooks
a division of Baker Publishing Group
Grand Rapids, Michigan

CHRIST
CHURCH
PRESS

Published by Baker Books
a division of Baker Publishing Group
Grand Rapids, Michigan
BakerBooks.com

Library of Congress Cataloging-in-Publication Data
Library of Congress Control Number 2025941178
ISBN 9781540906007 (paper)
ISBN 9781493465323 (ebook)

Lexham Editorial: Todd Hains, Jonathan Gardner, Danielle Burlaga, Mandi Newell
Cover Design: Gabriel Eason
Typesetting: Justin Marr

Baker Publishing Group publications use paper produced from sustainable forestry practices and postconsumer waste whenever possible.

26 27 28 29 30 31 32 7 6 5 4 3 2 1

To the Lims and Van Hofwegens
God is faithful.

"Fear not, little flock, for it is the Father's good pleasure to give you the kingdom."
—Luke 12:32

CONTENTS

PRAYER FOR CHRIST TO BE OUR TEACHER

IN THE NAME of the Father and of the Son and of the Holy Spirit. Amen.

May our sons in their youth
be like plants full grown,
our daughters like corner pillars
cut for the structure of a palace. *(Ps 144:12)*

For you, O Lord, are my hope,
my trust, O LORD, from my youth.
Upon you I have leaned from before my birth;
you are he who took me from my mother's womb.
My praise is continually of you. *(Ps 71:5–6)*

GRACIOUS FATHER, who satisfies the longings of parents, grant as the teacher of their children your own Son, the one in whom are hidden all the treasures of wisdom and knowledge. He utters to them dark sayings of old, telling the generation to come the glorious deeds of the Lord and the wonders he has done. Impart to our little ones not mere human wisdom but the wisdom and speech of your Spirit, that they may know the depths of his love. We praise and bless you that the kingdom of this world has become the kingdom of your Christ, who lives and reigns with you and the Holy Spirit, one God, now and forever. Amen.

Colossians 2:3
Psalm 78:2–4
1 Corinthians 2:13
Revelation 11:15

PROLOGUE

One Sunday morning after church, I overheard two dads talking in the lobby about how they had decided to read a book together about education: "We've gotta figure out how we are going to educate our kids." I too had five young children at the time and so (uninvited) I inserted myself. It quickly became clear to us how important this topic was, and by the end of our second meeting we had decided we would start a school. We had no idea what was involved in such an endeavor, but that didn't stop us from making ourselves a school board and pitching the idea to our church's elders.

That was twelve years ago, and during the time since, we have experienced in countless ways God's faithfulness and love to his covenant children. By doing the actual work of learning, teaching, and tweaking, he has given us a clearer and clearer vision for a distinctly Christ-centered education. Not just a school with a Bible class and believing teachers, but a school where the very educational philosophy and pedagogy is Christian through and through.

Our breakfast meetings began by learning about classical education, the way Christians have done education for many centuries. Many modern classical schools were also Christian. But we often found that these schools had trouble truly letting the gospel shape everything that they were doing. It was like classical and Christian were two friends that got along well. But the connection is deeper and more organic than that. The gospel is the seed and classical education is the natural fruit that grows out from it; the DNA of the one generates the other.

But as we have gone through the great challenges of making our church school (Trinity Classical School in Bellingham, Washington), we have come to see the power of having Christ at the center of everything we do. The vision laid down in this book has been forged through the furnace of building a school from the ground up. For anyone who has done it, they know the challenges. We have had such amazing people who have poured so much of their lives into our school. But even more, we've found over and over Jesus wisely shaping—in deep and beautiful ways—every aspect of the school's life.

It is easy for a pastor or head of school to say, "It's all about Jesus," and have that be an empty phrase parroted from someone else. This book is my attempt to show how truly the whole purpose of a school is to form the love of Christ in students, and the whole purpose of learning is to discover that everything holds together in Jesus. "All things were created through him and for him. And he is before all things, and in him all things hold together" (Col 1:16–17). One of the most important things Christians can do in our generation is recapture this vision for education and implement it in schools and communities all over the world. I have been so grateful to experience what God is doing in the movement of classical, Christian schools, and I pray that the vision for gospel education would encourage more and more people to become a part of this great work of the Spirit. The Lord our God who creates, redeems, sanctifies, and teaches bless your children with a beautiful vision of God's undeterred grace in every domain of human existence.

Nate Walker
Pentecost 2024

INTRODUCTION

Lord, help me to do great things as though they were little, since I do them with your power, and little things as though they were great, since I do them in your name.

Blaise Pascal, *Pensées*

EDUCATION BRINGS TOGETHER things great and small. Children (small things) learn about history, theology, math, science, and God (great things). We educate after the pattern of our Teacher. He who was great became small in Jesus Christ so that those who are small might become great in him.

For parents, there are two deep loves—one small and one great—that should guide our approach to thinking about our child's education. The first love is only called small because, well, what is smaller than a kindergartener? By the time your child is a kindergartener, you've had several years to learn about her personality and interests, gifts and weaknesses. You know she's a unique image-bearer of God, and you long for these qualities to blossom and flourish. In his wisdom, God has given parents a singular love for their own children that mirrors the faithful care and attention he gives to us. What a beautiful thing. Though our culture has either devalued children or else gone too far in idolizing them, Christian realism about our children's faults shouldn't diminish in the least the value we see in them and the good we want for them. It's a reflection of our Father's goodness toward us when we as parents have such great love for such small things as our children.

But Christians throughout history have not let this singular love for our children be the only love that shapes our vision for their education. The small must be paired with the great. Education grossly fails if it only dotes on the child or indulges the child's desires for autonomy. Those charming little kindergarteners must be brought from the kingdom of darkness to the kingdom of light. They must be trained as faithful and useful servants of the Most High God.

The history of the world is about the great conflict between the City of God and the City of Man. This rivalry, first seen in the violence of Cain against his brother Abel, was the same rivalry that placed Jesus on a cross. World history is about the kingdoms of this world becoming the kingdom of the crucified and risen King (Rev 11:15). Our children are citizens of heaven, placed on earth as representatives of their homeland and of this King. Their minds must be well trained in the laws, stories, customs, and traditions of the heavenly capital city where their hearts find their identity.

It's common for Bible-believing American Christians to criticize those who practice "cultural Christianity." The idea is that being a Christian is about having a personal relationship with Christ, so simply living in a Christian culture should not make someone presume they are saved. I sympathize with this train of thought and absolutely affirm that Christ intended for each of his people to know him personally, with hearts that trust in his forgiving grace. But in our day, as the Christian influence in our society erodes, we may be ready to appreciate that Christianity is itself a culture.[1] It doesn't simply fight culture or even transform culture. It is a culture. It always has been. We have our own ways of thinking and speaking and acting—our own stories and art and traditions and practices. We have our own understanding of history and the meaning of life. Even when we share the same language and manners and histories as our neighbors, there's something else true about our shared Christian culture that transcends our earthly cultural differences. That something else—everything that makes up our heavenly culture—Jesus gives us to form us as a people for God's own possession (as 1 Pet 2:9 puts it).

St. Augustine referred to this culture as the City of God and recognized that the City of God is always (for now, at least) intermingled with the City of Man. The City of Man finds its way into the church, just as the City of God finds its way into the broader culture.

But it must be understood by Christians that God's plan, revealed throughout the Bible, is to build a civilization on the earth where he is honored as King. Jesus teaches us to pray, "Your kingdom come, your will be done, on earth as it is in heaven" (Matt 6:10). The kingdom of God is not simply a place our souls go when we die, but heaven has invaded earth with the coming of Christ and the sending of the Spirit. God's kingdom is a civilization he is establishing on the earth. It is currently two billion members strong in every nation.[2] This civilization has outlived the Babylonian Empire, the Roman Empire, and the

Ottoman Empire. It will outlive the United States of America, China, and Russia. There has never been and never will be an Emperor like Jesus. "May his name endure forever, his fame continue as long as the sun!" (Ps 72:17).

So our vision of education must bring together small and great things. The small thing is a parent who wants above all things for his or her child to know the love of Christ and to behold his glory in all things. Education is deeply personal in this sense. But Christian families must also place this small vision in the context of the bigger vision: Jesus is building a multinational civilization on the earth. Our children are a part of that kingdom, and he has plans for them to help in his kingdom building.

What are those traditions and customs of the City of God to which we as Christians pledge allegiance? These traditions have already been finding their way into the cultures of the earth over the course of history. When we've been faithful to proclaim and to follow the Word of our King, the City of God has been the source of sound thinking, just laws, beautiful arts, robust theology, invention, discipline, and virtue. Our city has been marked by two great commandments: loving God with all our heart, soul, strength, and mind; and loving our neighbors as ourselves (Matt 22:37–40).

When we begin to understand that the purpose of education is to train children as redeemed citizens of the city whose two laws are love of God and love of neighbor, the main argument of this book will start to become clear: Education is Jesus forming children in love. You might think of it in terms of the following line of reasoning:

> Educational formation is the foundation of any civilization.
> Jesus is building a civilization ruled by love.

Therefore, Christian education is primarily about a child being formed in the love of Jesus.

History shows that at every key step in the growth of God's kingdom, the education of common people has been an essential component. Whether it was the prolific book production of the early church, the monasteries that converted Western Europe and brought learning to the barbarians, the cathedral and court schools under the education reforms of Charlemagne and Alfred the Great, the universities of medieval Europe, the many schools during and after the Reformation that brought literacy to the masses so they could read and understand the Word of God for themselves, or the missionary schools of the last century that have brought learning to people of every nation to help lift them out of poverty and empower them to transform their communities: Christian education built the Western world and has brought the love and light of Christ to every nation through missions.

Why have Christians pursued this education-based approach to being and building God's kingdom? Because Jesus made education central to his plan for world transformation: "Go therefore and make disciples of all nations, baptizing them in the name of the Father and of the Son and of the Holy Spirit, teaching them to observe all that I have commanded" (Matt 28:19–20). Jesus's plan is simple: baptize and teach. If we believe in the lordship of Jesus over all of life, then the Great Commission is not just about obeying Jesus in "spiritual" matters but seeing every area of life and learning as a spiritual matter and, therefore, all of education as an experience of discipleship.

The heart of the City of God is shaped through worship, but the mind is shaped through education. Discipleship is education. And in fact, all education is also discipleship. Jesus tells the church to disciple the nations, but who is currently discipling the children of the American church? Unfortunately, it is not the church. Secular government schools and the onslaught of media content are given far more formative hours in the lives of Christian children than the church. We have experienced a massive hemorrhaging of Christian children from the church. Statistics say that as many as two-thirds of children growing up in the church have left by the time they are adults,[3] and Christians bemoan the loss of cultural influence they experience in modern society.

We might be tempted to blame the unbelieving culture around us for this. More honest reflection would lead us to consider that the American church has lost her heritage of civilization building through worship and learning. Maybe we've narrowed the faith to simply being about going to heaven when you die. Or maybe we have not appreciated how thoroughly the lordship of Christ applies to all of life.

How does a school pursue this educational mission in our day? History again proves that the Christian education generated by the gospel looks like the classical tradition of the liberal arts.

Though I've divided this book into two sections, The Gospel and Classical Education, my argument is not that schools should add Jesus to the liberal arts to Christianize them. Instead, this whole book is about the gospel and what it alone can accomplish. It is about the redeeming love of Christ for a sinful and rebellious world, one which he is making new through making disciples. I aim to show that the shape of classical education (the liberal arts and sciences, training in wisdom, the great books of Western civilization, and cultivating an imaginative mind in beauty, goodness, and truth) is a natural outflow of a culture that believes the gospel of Jesus Christ. The powerful Word of the gospel creates the reality it announces; when it comes to education, century after century, Christians have found that the kind of education the gospel produces is a classical one.

This book is not a how-to manual for organizing a Christian school (although I hope it helps those who take on such a worthy task). I intend this book to be a manifesto: an inspiring vision of God's gospel purposes for education as a whole and a plan for how to think through applying that vision in several areas of classical study. Jesus is the greatest teacher in history. This book is for the disciples—and the disciple-makers—whom he has formed in love by the gospel and who desire to form godly children in turn. And my hope is that, through Christ, we'll experience a beautiful marriage of the great and the small.

When we looked at God's wisdom, we saw something of His mind; when we thought of His power, we saw something of His hand and His arm; when we considered His word, we learned about His mouth; but now, contemplating His love, we are to look into His heart.

J. I. Packer, *Knowing God*

1

THE COVENANT CHILD

"The most important thing I have to realize is that my children are not mine. The most important relationship in their life is not their relationship with me but their relationship with God. I find this so comforting." A friend with older children said this to me recently as he was reflecting on his experience as a parent. This friend has been very thoughtful about passing his faith on to his children—they love God. But my friend also said he has known Christians who do not seem to rest in the truth that God loves our children more than we do. This leads to anxiety about raising kids in a hostile world instead of confidence in Christ our King.

Like those anxious parents, Christian schools are often criticized for having a fortress mentality. Such institutions see the world as a dark and godless place, and so their defensive hearts lead them to lock their children in safe havens, holding out until the spiritual war in the world is finally over. This mentality isn't totally wrong; children are vulnerable and need protection. But the image of a fortress school—its children surrounded by an iron wall so tall they can't even see the wider world, much less engage with it—isn't exactly the trusting, nurturing, empowering educational environment a mother dreams of for her babies. The question is, do we really think such an environment is what God wants for these children he loves even more than we do?

If children need protection, but the iron walls of a man-made fortress simply won't do—what then? What comes to mind for me is a school with God's giant arms encircling it—like the arms of a father, with children playing and singing and learning and loving within them—his delighted face looking on with pleasure. Sometimes the children are aware of these invisible arms but generally not. Like most of us, they are oblivious to God's continual providence. But always, there is a subconscious sense within them that God is present and he is caring for them. A father's arms should protect his children. But more importantly, these arms should wrestle and tickle and throw them in the air and catch them every time. God is a fortress (Ps 62:2), but a fortress of love and joy. That's the pattern for parenting and for schooling because it's the pattern for living as human beings in relationship with God and one another.

OUR COVENANT GOD

God's arms do have some parallels to an encircling fortress, then, but only as a byproduct of gathering his children and keeping them close. A school begins when God places his strong and loving arms around the children of his people and says, "Within these arms, you will grow to think and feel and speak and act and laugh. And above all, you will learn to follow me."

So what exactly are these invisible arms of God that form the life of a Christian school? The Bible's word for God's nurturing and protecting embrace is covenant. A covenant is a committed relationship built on promises. It is especially God's promise to make us his people and be faithful to us. It's like a wedding vow. When a man and a woman say to each other, "I will never leave you," those vows act like arms around the marriage. All the love and fighting, sin and affection, happen within the security of those arms, holding two sinners together and saying, "Whatever happens, we're committed to each other." A husband wraps his arms around his wife and children; a wedding ring wraps around a finger as a sign of their marriage covenant. God's covenant is like a shelter or a covering that he places over his people. It's the thing that, despite conflict on the outside and sin on the inside, cannot be shaken.

God makes his covenant promises to his people's children, too. Before God told Abraham to give his children a Christian education (Gen 18:19), he first promised in Genesis 17:7, "I will establish my covenant between me and you and your offspring after you throughout their generations for an everlasting covenant, to be God to you and to your offspring after you." Christian education builds on this rock-solid covenant foundation.

Now you know why we're starting a book on education by going deep into God's covenant-making and covenant-keeping heart. How can a school be a training center for Christian love without relying on the faithful covenant presence of Love himself?

The Bible seems to know we have a tendency to skip this part of the Christian life. Like a repeated chorus in a song, God sings his covenant promises to our families over and over again throughout the Bible so we won't forget: "I will be a God to you and to your children." He sang it to Abraham. He sang about thousands of generations to Moses (Exod 20:6; 34:7; Deut 7:9). He sang it to David and Solomon (2 Sam 7:12–16); he sang it to the exiles in Babylon (Jer 30:22; Ezek 36:28). He (literally) sang about our children's children in the Psalms (Ps 128:6).

That song was taken up by Jesus himself: "Let the children come to me, and do not hinder them, for to such belongs the kingdom of God" (Luke 18:16). Our Lord wrapped his arms around the children of God's people and blessed them. The divine arms of the Old Testament covenant became the flesh and blood arms of our Savior.

The Bible everywhere considers that the children among God's people are to be treated as full-fledged members of God's household. The children of believers have been born into that covenant relationship built on promises that God has made with their parents. These promises continue seamlessly from the Old Testament into the New. On the day of Pentecost, the apostle Peter reaffirmed God's covenant promise that had already endured for so many centuries:

> Repent and be baptized every one of you in the name of Jesus Christ for the forgiveness of your sins, and you will receive the gift of the Holy Spirit. For the promise is for you and for your children and for all who are far off, everyone whom the Lord our God calls to himself. (Acts 2:38–39)

The apostle Paul addresses children in his letters to the New Testament churches (Eph 6:1; Col 3:20), calling them "saints" along with everyone else (Eph 1:1; Col 1:2). He considers them joint heirs together with their parents and all adult believers (1 Cor 7:14). Grace, by God's design, is meant to flow down the lines of generations. Faith in Christ is a "tradition" (2 Thess 2:15) that we pass down from father to daughter, mother to son (2 Tim 1:5). Treasure these promises to all Christian parents as we struggle through the hard work of raising our kids in the Lord.

God's covenant promises to our children are the foundation of a Christian school and the basis for our children's education and discipleship. They give children a protection rooted in love and not in fear. These promises should be the hope and treasure of any Christian parent. Our kids aren't more righteous than other kids; they struggle with all the same sins. But God has surrounded our children with the loving arms of his promise and brought them into his covenant of love. By simply placing our children in the homes of believing parents, he has already done an incredible act of grace in their lives.

A CHILD'S FAITH

To be clear, God's covenant promise does not mean that our children are automatically saved because they grow up in Christian homes. Covenants are committed relationships; God's covenant requires our children to embrace his promises for themselves. Though the Bible everywhere considers our children as included among the people of God, they are also given responsibilities as covenant members. The first and most important of these responsibilities is to believe—to receive and rest in his promises by faith.

The majority of children in the church, when offered the gospel in an age-appropriate way, will profess faith at a very young age. Jesus anticipated this when he said in Luke 18 to let the little children come to him. So we should regularly give our children opportunities to profess their faith, and we should celebrate young faith when we see it. A miracle has happened! The Holy Spirit has worked faith in their young hearts. Praise God!

We can be tempted to look on young faith with suspicion or distrust. "Are you just saying you believe because your parents told you to answer in a certain way?" Let's not be so cynical. Of course, Christian children believe because their parents told them to—that's how God intended they should learn about Jesus and be saved! Whether it was Abraham or us, God planned that we would preach the gospel to our children and they would hear it and believe. Questioning the maturity or sincerity of a child's faith has the real potential of poisoning their understanding of the gospel, suggesting to them that salvation can be earned by becoming more sophisticated in their understanding of the truth. We might unintentionally communicate that our children are saved by being more spiritually mature or fruitful instead of being saved by Jesus through sheer mercy received by simple faith. Let's give them assurance in the good news of God's grace, which is the true motivation for spiritual growth.

The beauty of God's covenant for parents is that it frees us to water the young faith of our children by pouring on them the amazing promises of God. Some Christian parents feel reluctant to assure their children of God's promises too freely. Yet these are the very promises that must nurture the faith of any believer, young or old. Promises like these:

+ You were chosen in love by God before the world began (Eph 1:4).
+ You have been bought by the precious blood of Jesus (1 Cor 7:23).
+ You have the Holy Spirit living inside of you as God's guarantee to you that you are God's beloved child (Eph 1:13–14).
+ Your sins are washed away, not by your good works but by grace through faith (Eph 2:8–9).
+ You are God's craftsmanship, and he has planned all your good works for you so you simply need to walk in them (Eph 2:10).

+ No one can snatch you from your Father's hand or Jesus's hand (John 10:28–29).

+ You are a member of God's family; God has adopted you, and all the people at church are your mothers, fathers, brothers, and sisters (1 Tim 3:15; Rom 8:14–15).

+ You will spend all eternity in the presence of God and fellow believers in a renewed creation with no more tears or sorrow (Rev 21:1–4).

Christian children should know these promises like the sound of their mother's voice. These promises create an unshakable identity for a covenant child.

Children come into the world looking to their parents (and then their teachers and peers) to answer for them, "Who am I?" The modern world lays on them an impossible burden by answering, "You can be anybody you want to be! You get to create yourself!" That sounds incredible—until you actually try it. It doesn't work. We weren't made to make ourselves. Our culture is asking children to do the work only God can do: the creation of a person in his image. But in the covenant promise of the gospel, each of our children receives his or her personal identity as a gift of grace. Each Christian child is a son or daughter of God in Christ and a sinner saved by grace, set apart for good works and destined for glory.

The Christian school is fruitful as it grows in the fertile soil of God's grace. Children should grow up feeling his promises surrounding and upholding them. They should sense it in their teachers and hear about it constantly in chapel. They should feel secure, loved, and free and should sense deeply that they know who they are in Christ.

THE PARENTS' RESPONSIBILITY

God's covenant always consists of both promises and responsibilities. One of these responsibilities is for children to believe, as already mentioned. But what about parents? When God made a covenant with Abraham and his children, he gave clear instructions to Abraham on how to raise them: "For I have chosen him, that he may command his children and his household after him to keep the way of the Lord by doing righteousness and justice" (Gen 18:19). The children receive their identity as a gift from God ("I have chosen"), but they also must be taught how to live in accord with that identity ("that he may command"). The same is true for us today.

The Christian school will never replace the essential role of parents in the formation of children. But the school can be a great help to parents in this daunting task. Part of the way God shows covenant grace to parents is in providing a covenant community to support us in discipling our children. Parenting is hard. We don't have to do it alone.

My family loves to discuss Bible passages around the dinner table. We cover only a little ground at any one time because one verse often leads to a half-hour discussion. I prefer these free-form talks exploring my children's reflections and insights, rather than drilling them on the Westminster Shorter Catechism. But I also know systematic instruction in the fundamentals of theology is of immense benefit to maturing Christians. It equips them to have such in-depth, free-form discussions in the first place. I'm grateful that our school helps me to fulfill my responsibilities as a Christian parent, especially in areas where I struggle or don't have time or expertise.

At the same time, I love to focus on teaching my kids to play tennis, go backpacking, or make home movies. Knowing that the school has algebra and Latin covered frees me to be the fun dad. A child needs to be taught innumerable lessons growing up in God's wild and complex creation. The school specializes in several crucial areas—writing, reading, math, history, and so on—so that parents can have the joyful task of introducing them to the rest of life.

But I must insist again: The Bible clearly gives the responsibility to disciple Christian children to parents.

> These words that I command you today shall be on your heart. You shall teach them diligently to your children, and shall talk of them when you sit in your house, and when you walk by the way, and when you lie down, and when you rise. You shall bind them as a sign on your hand, and they shall be as frontlets between your eyes. You shall write them on the doorposts of your house and on your gates. (Deut 6:6–9)

The whole day of a child should be surrounded by the truth of God and his Word because all of life is lived to glorify God and obey him. God's Word can't stay confined to Sunday mornings; it must come up in the normal, everyday events of home life. Again, the New Testament echoes these instructions to parents:

> Fathers, do not provoke your children to anger, but bring them up in the discipline and instruction of the Lord. (Eph 6:4)

The word translated as "discipline" in this verse is the Greek word *paideia*. In the ancient Greek world, *paideia* was about more than simply correcting a child when he disobeyed. It was the whole structure of home, school, community, and civic life that prepared a child to become an ideal citizen in the ancient world—or even more, the ideal man.[1]

Jesus, too, is building a new civilization (the kingdom of God) with citizens from every nation and a culture formed by God's

Word and the community of faith. How will our children learn to live as citizens of that great kingdom? Notice Paul's focus on fathers in Ephesians 6:4. Paul told the fathers of the Ephesian church to form a school, culture, and communal life (a *paideia*) centered on the person of Jesus. They are not supposed to simply correct disobedient children (as important as that is). They are to train them in the ways of Jesus's kingdom.

As parents, therefore, we should rest in the promises God has given to our children to be their God, just as he is ours. But we must also recognize that we are God's appointed means for our children's discipleship. Just as a Christian who neglects going to church can't expect to grow in his faith, so we can't expect our children to love God if we don't obey God's command to disciple them.

Second only to the Holy Spirit, parents have by far the greatest influence on the faith of their children. There are few things more powerful than a child growing up every week at church seeing her mom faithfully listening to the sermon or her dad singing to the Lord with conviction. Coming together as a family every week to receive God's Word and approach the Lord's Table deeply shapes the identity of everyone in the family, not least our children. They learn that God's house is their home. Even if they wander at some point in their life, the comfort of the church will always be a draw to them.

This doesn't mean parents will be perfect in their discipleship. Far from it. Any parent knows the countless ways our sin muddies our childrearing—yelling, anger, impatience, selfishness, and many other sins are all still at work in us. But even in the mess of parenting mistakes, our children should see the grace of Jesus. His love and power are the only hope that can hold our families together. Let our children see the Bible as the thing that humbled their dad so that he admitted his sin and apologized. Let them see the gospel of forgiveness motivate warring siblings to reconcile. Homes are rarely peaceful, and if there ever is peace, they can be sure it came from Jesus.

So, the starting place for any school that trains children in love is the promise of God's covenant, beautifully expressed in the welcome of Jesus: "Let the little children come to me." We are only ready to form little humans in Christian schools when we have internalized these promises as the source of our children's identity (together with our own) in Christian homes.

Jesus thou joy of loving hearts,
Thou Fount of life, thou Light of men,
From the best bliss that earth imparts
We turn unfilled to thee again.

Bernard of Clairvaux

2

A GOSPEL CULTURE

Once we understand that God's covenant love is the foundation of a Christian education, we can begin to think through how that love must permeate the life and culture of a school community. We call this a gospel culture.

G. K. Chesterton considered "the great lesson of 'the Beauty and the Beast'" to be one of the fundamental laws of the universe: "A thing must be loved before it is lovable."[1] Chesterton first learned this in fairy tales but then came to find its origin in Christianity: "We love because he first loved us" (1 John 4:19). There is no more important principle for the formation of children as they grow up and prepare to live in God's world. They must be loved before they can become lovable. In a school with a gospel culture, this principle permeates not only the teaching and chapel talks but the very way the community relates to one another among faculty, staff, students, and parents. Gospel-fueled love should be the mood of the school; you should sense it as soon as you spend even a day there.

Our school has translated Chesterton's fundamental law into this gospel principle: God loves me perfectly in Christ, therefore I want to obey him.

This principle is not just a spiritual statement about a person's relationship to God. This principle is based on the gospel's power to shape the whole culture and atmosphere of a school. We hope it will be the very air that our children breathe for the thirteen years of their primary and secondary education. It is the heart of a Christian education in love.

We can also think about a school's culture as its personality. What will a school be like as it is shaped by this principle of grateful obedience, fueled by God's love in Christ? Let's first consider what it shouldn't be like.

TWO DISTORTED GOSPEL CULTURES

We can contrast the true gospel, and a school culture or personality that flows from it, with two alternatives—each a subtle but serious distortion of it. Both alternatives miss the heart of the gospel in a fundamental way, and both give rise to a certain distorted personality within a school committed to being Christian—so we must all be on guard.

The first distorted personality is Legalist, whose inner dialogue reverses the two sides of the gospel principle: If I obey God, then he will love me.

Take a moment to re-read that principle, imagining a community that operates according to its logic. What words come to mind to describe its atmosphere? Perhaps words like fear, shame, pride, arrogance, self-righteousness, hiding, fakeness, isolation, judgment. Many people instinctively distrust religious schools, and often, the reason is that they have experienced the suffocating personality of Legalist. Imagining our children in such a culture thirty hours per week throughout their childhood should be frightening! Jesus warned his disciples about Legalist's poison whenever he criticized the Pharisees. We are right to run from the same danger.

Yet the difference between legalism and the gospel is subtle. There are many churches and schools whose statements of faith clearly confess the gospel while the culture nevertheless feels legalistic. A truly gospel-centered school doesn't merely grasp the gospel intellectually; the very mood of the school is captivated and motivated by the grace of Jesus.

Why does Legalist create such a rigid and distant school culture? Because he views God in primarily rule-based terms. Legalist believes that God's main interest is in us passing a test or obeying a set of requirements. God's deepest concern is whether we measure up and how well we perform. Of course, God's relationship to us is legal, just like a marriage is legal. His covenant promises are written in the Bible like a legal document, and he gives us laws that guide us in walking with him. But his laws are not an end in themselves. The laws serve the relationship, not the other way around. Legalist does not understand this.

How different is legalism from the gospel, which says that what God primarily wants for us is communion with him—that we would be in the Father as Jesus is in the Father! That is what we were made for, and that is why he is saving us. He wants us to know him and love him. He wants a relationship. Therefore, if education is about forming a child in love, then the school must be vigilant in guarding against the influence of Legalist.

Many people in the current generation, in fact, have recognized the corrosive effect of legalism. But in the process of resisting legalism, they've sometimes fallen into another distorted personality that is equally harmful: Lawless, whose inner dialogue runs like this: God loves me perfectly; therefore, I don't need to obey.

On the surface, it may sound like Lawless believes in an extreme form of grace because she insists on only hearing about God's acceptance. But the god of Lawless is equally as hard as the god of Legalist. Why can't she hear about God's commandments? Why can't she bear him convicting her of sin? Only because, deep down, she doesn't believe he is really good and gracious. She doesn't trust him. The heart of Lawless hears any commandment from God and it immediately produces an unbearable shame in her. Any mention of sin and she rebuffs, "Don't burden me with judgment!" The lawless one who won't submit to God's commandments or turn from sin is actually keeping God at a distance. In her heart is a deep insecurity in her relationship to God. The only reason she plugs her ears to God's commands and objects, "Grace, grace, grace!" is because grace hasn't actually given peace to her heart. She doesn't really know that God's commandments aren't burdensome (1 John 5:3) and that the Lord is "faithful and just" not only "to forgive us our sins" but also "to cleanse us from all unrighteousness" (1 John 1:9).

What words would describe a school culture built on the false freedom and spiritual insecurity of lawlessness? Disorder, selfishness, injustice, chaos, childishness, rudeness, anxiety, and lack of repentance. There is little reverence for Christ and weak love for God. While we certainly don't want to immerse our children in a culture of legalism, is lawlessness any better?

Deep down, neither Legalist nor Lawless experiences true communion with the living and loving God. Legalist is constantly burdened by guilt; Lawless is constantly running from it. But neither have truly had their guilt washed by the grace of Christ. Only the heart shaped by the gospel can intimately come to know God. Only the gospel can train a young heart in love and move that heart to love not only in word but in deed.

A TRUE GOSPEL CULTURE

So what words would describe the personality of a community truly built on the gospel—whose name is neither Legalist nor Lawless but Love? Joy, compassion, humility, trust, intimacy, confession, wonder, forgiveness, reconciliation, community, gentleness, worship. What a beautiful environment! But we must also add holiness and obedience to this list. You might think holiness and obedience sound like things that are the specialty of Legalist. Not true. True holiness and obedience only come from the heart, and only the gospel can create a heart that brings forth the fruit of the Spirit.

Our vision must be for covenant children to breathe the air of the gospel every day of their childhood, and by breathing that air, they will learn to love the way Jesus does. They will learn security and assurance; they will learn trust, relationship, and humility. The gospel is the only thing that can both train us in love and give us the love it requires of us.

How is such a culture created? It must begin with the spiritual formation of the parents, teachers, and staff. They set the culture of the school, and the mood of the school will reflect the hearts of these adults. Have these adults had their own guilt met with the grace of Jesus? Do they have the fruit of the Spirit formed in them through weekly gospel-centered worship, personal meditation on the Word of God, confession, and prayer? Parents and teachers must taste grace themselves before they can feed it to their children and students.

That is the first part of the gospel principle: God loves me perfectly in Christ. But what about the second part: Therefore, I want to obey? Obedience to God's law isn't divorced from the gospel; it's the grace-enabled way we render our gratitude to him for his abundant love. In a Christian school, God's law is largely communicated through the school's rules.

SCHOOL RULES AND THE GOSPEL

A gospel culture in a school is not only formed by a proper understanding of the gospel but also a proper understanding of how rules work. Rules are an application of God's law into the orderly life of the student body. So, to understand school rules in particular, we have to see them in light of the purpose of God's law in general. Historically, Christians have said there are three purposes or "uses" for God's law:

+ To show us our sin and drive us to Christ
+ To prevent abuse and mistreatment
+ To guide us in living like Jesus

Let's apply each of these to the role of rules in the Christian school.

Rules are meant to drive students again and again to Christ. A Christian school should never be surprised that its students are sinners. If you think you can protect children from sin by putting them in a Christian school, you're kidding yourself. They bring the sin in with them. It shouldn't shock us to find lying, cheating, bullying, laziness, disrespect, and pride among our students. The rules will expose these sins and, like a mirror, show the students what's buried in their hearts.

This is the point where a gospel school starts to diverge so clearly from the legalistic or lawless school. Legalism believes that rules can change the heart. But the gospel school knows rules don't take away sin; only Jesus does. Every occasion when a rule exposes sin in the heart of a student becomes an opportunity to lead him or her back to Jesus. Thousands of times, sin will arise in the life of a school, each instance becoming a divine appointment to share and believe the gospel anew.

Will these opportunities turn into lectures about doing better or even lectures shaming a child already torn up with guilt? Or will the teacher or administrator or parent use these opportunities to train a child in repentance? How do you turn from sin and receive the grace of Jesus?

To be clear, preaching the gospel to students rarely means converting them to Christ in the popular sense of the term. The great majority of these children are professing Christians. My point is, we Christians need to hear and believe the gospel just as much as non-Christians do. We always need to hear that Jesus is a friend to sinners and God accepts us not because of our good works but because of Jesus's good works on our behalf. The same is true for our Christian students. Martin Luther said that repentance is a lifetime project for all of us.[2]

How can rules lead us to the gospel? Imagine a young boy has just hit another student on the playground. The perpetrator is brought to the administrator's office. The first questions the administrator must ask herself is, "Is his heart hard or soft? Is the student still proud or has he been humbled?" If he is proud, then he needs more law to expose his sin so he can recognize his guilt and feel the legitimate shame of it. God's law is given to humble the proud. But often, a child in the principal's office or in the hall with a teacher knows his sin already. He might feel fear or shame or embarrassment. This child needs the gospel. The administrator should say, "When you hit your friend, you were not acting like a loved child who loves others. You have forgotten how loved you are by your heavenly Father. You know what you did was very wrong. Who is the only One who can take away your sin?" When he says,

"Jesus," and he is reminded of the good news of the cross, he should then be asked, "And do you trust Jesus to take away your sin and to keep his promises to save you and send his Holy Spirit to help you?"

Now, at this moment, when we as administrators or teachers or parents ask children this question, we should be holding our breath as we wait for the answer. What will they say? Their answer matters. When they say yes, they trust Jesus, and we should feel a jolt of joy in our hearts. Faith is the work of the Spirit! Their young trust means God's love is living in them. Tell them that. Celebrate with them. They should be sent back into the playground with appropriate consequences but also prayed for and assured of God's gospel promises. This is how we train children in repentance motivated by grace.

Some of you might think me pedantic for detailing all this. But I suspect others are glad for the practical direction! Either way, gospel conversations that sound more or less like this must happen over and over again in any Christian school that intends to be gospel-centered not just on paper but in its culture. Grace cannot be taken for granted. We can't assume the gospel with our students—we must give it to them. If we need to hear about the forgiveness and grace of Jesus over and over again, then so do they.

I recognize this conversation can't happen every time a student breaks a rule over the course of the school day. Nonetheless, in the home and in the school, this should be a conversation held countless times over the course of a Christian childhood. The most familiar words to covenant children should be God, sin, Jesus, cross, trust, forgiveness, and the Holy Spirit. This is the grammar of the gospel. It's the only language that can bring lasting peace after a playground fight or genuine submission from a rebellious troublemaker or new hope to a student caught cheating.

So first, we must see the rules of the school as God's way of driving young people to the grace of Christ. But this is not the only reason God has given our students rules to live by.

Rules protect the weak in a school from all forms of abuse and neglect. As we've seen, the lawless school cannot be a safe place because there is no order or obedience. Children do not thrive in chaos. The legalist school isn't the only place students can be mistreated. Dallas Willard has described many modern school playgrounds with sobering words:

> Hardened, lonely little souls, ready for addiction, aggression, isolation, self-destructive behavior, and for some, even extreme violence, go out to mingle their madness with one another in nightmarish school grounds and "communities." ... The wonder is not that they sometimes destroy one another, but that the adults who produced them and live with them can, with apparent sincerity, ask, "Why?"[3]

The law of God is meant to protect vulnerable souls (and bodies) from such assault. This means there is a sense in which the rules of the school should create fear in the students. God is a protector of the weak, and if you intend to hurt the weak, it is right that you should fear him. That might translate to a healthy fear of the Head of School, too. God's law in the Bible threatens the wicked not only to show them their need of grace but to curb the injustice in their hearts from flowing out in wicked words and deeds. Students should know that if they bully younger children or disrespect the adults serving and caring for them, there will be serious consequences.

Rules aren't contrary to the gospel, then, because they demonstrate Jesus's loving protection of those under his care. The King is present in the walls of the Christian school and his children should feel safe in his love. Rules reinforce this sense of security and make tangible the justice of Jesus's kingly rule. John Stott has noted that children respect the exercise of justice and recognize it as in harmony with love:

> If they have done something that they know is wrong, they also know that they deserve punishment, and they both expect and want to receive it. They also know at once if the punishment is being administered either without love or contrary to justice. The two most poignant cries of a child are "Nobody loves me" and "It isn't fair." Their sense of love and justice comes from God, who made them in his image and who revealed himself as holy love at the cross.[4]

This second protective purpose for rules needs to be treated carefully. Schools can become tyrannical in their rule-making, and a sense of fear and constraint can come to dominate any sense of love and freedom. How do we avoid this imbalance? Here are three rules of thumb:

+ Root every rule in love. The law of God is summarized in love. When we make a rule, can we clearly show that it is an expression of love for God and neighbor? Can students feel that every rule is softened by love? "Clothe naked statute with love's soft array."[5]

+ Root every rule in the Bible. Don't "go beyond what is written" (1 Cor 4:6). Of course, schools have to create rules that aren't explicitly named in

God's Word, but to make sure the school's rules (or a home's rules) don't become burdensome, it's always wise to ask ourselves, "Is this actually required or forbidden by God in the Bible?"

+ Avoid multiplying rules. God's law can be summarized in ten general commandments that apply in some way or another to every aspect of life. It's a very human temptation to multiply rules in an attempt to control others (and, sometimes, to justify ourselves). Especially as students grow into the upper grades, specific rules should be fewer; general principles of virtue should be their guide.

Rules based on God's Word and rooted in love will prove a blessing to both faculty and students, protecting a healthy gospel culture in the school. And this leads to the most important purpose of God's law and rules in the school.

Rules train children in godly love and virtue. The Christian faith teaches that love isn't primarily something we feel but something we do. Not just with our hearts but with our bodies. God did not just feel love for humanity; he came down in the flesh to love us in word and deed.

Carefully thought-out rules train children in this kind of embodied, practical love. While rules cannot change the heart of a sinner—only the grace of Jesus can do that, remember—once Jesus has begun to change a heart, that heart will long to learn how to love in meaningful ways.

In a gospel-centered classical school, following rules that train in love while avoiding both legalism and lawlessness will often look like practicing manners. Manners have a bad rap in our culture. Modern people think manners exist to dull individuality and kill spontaneity. But honestly, do you feel that way when you meet well-mannered people? Don't you rather find them charming, agreeable, and interesting? They are courteous, slow to speak, quick to listen; they stand when someone else enters the room and open the door for others out of respect and empathy. When you're speaking, they pay attention to you rather than to their phone.

Why do we feel so honored around people with manners? In his biography of St. Francis of Assisi, Chesterton said that Francis's life of poverty was colored with a delightful insistence on courtesy:

> We may say if we like that St. Francis, in the bare and barren simplicity of his life, had clung to one rag of luxury: the manners of a court. But whereas in a court there is one king and a hundred courtiers, in this story there was one courtier, moving among a hundred kings. For he treated the whole mob of men as a mob of kings.[6]

C. S. Lewis similarly wrote that medieval chivalry was largely a training in both courage and manners:

> The man who combines both characteristics—the knight—is a work not of nature but of art; of that art which has human beings, instead of canvas or marble, for its medium.[7]

We don't naturally bestow on everyone the honor normally reserved for those considered especially important. We don't naturally combine bravery and tact. The skills of love are never the results of a natural accident. They're an intentional work of art. This art should be a goal of rules in the school.

We'll see later that the liberal arts train students in goodness, beauty, and truth, and in this way, embodied virtue (the goal of manners) is essential to an education in love. Our world desperately needs a renewal in manners and civility, because manners are simply a way of training human beings to use our bodies to act out love.

A WORD ON WEAKNESS

There is always a tension in the Christian life between the demands of the law and the grace of the gospel. What is remarkable about the gospel is that God has found a way to be gracious to us in our weakness, without lowering the bar of the law's demands. Our Savior does not flinch when he says, "You therefore must be perfect, as your heavenly Father is perfect" (Matt 5:48). The good news is that Jesus did not just stay in heaven and make the demand: "Here is the bar—now you all meet it in your own strength!" Instead, he left heaven, came down to our level, and lowered himself below us, that he might lift us up in his own strength. He's like a kindergarten teacher coming down to the level of a child, helping him as he struggles to learn handwriting. That is grace—that doesn't lessen the perfect demands of God's good law but reaches down to us in our weakness to help us up. "My grace is sufficient for you, for my power is made perfect in weakness" (2 Cor 12:9).

A gospel school will follow the pattern of our Lord in this. We must be resolved to keep the high standards of hard work and gracious manners while building support structures that help weak students experience deep learning and even success. That asks a lot of teachers and administrators. My mother was a tutor for kids with special needs her whole career. One student interviewed her before accepting her help: "Have you ever had anyone run from the room screaming? That is what I did with my last tutor." She said, "No, I haven't." She was able to build a trusting relationship with him. He ended up bringing her to school for show-and-tell and later made sure she was at his high school graduation. There is hardly anything that will stir love in us like someone who was kind and helpful to us in our weakness.

Grace is different from empathy. Empathy feels for a person but leaves them where they are. Grace transforms. Grace is generous, patient, and respectful. But it doesn't bow to the demands of the weak. Teachers are like coaches. Great coaches are not empathetic. They are encouraging but are always expecting more out of us and believing we can do it ("easy to please, hard to satisfy"). Our current culture of empathy is so afraid of a child feeling shame at his failure that standards continue to be lowered. The gospel instead says, "You are not meeting the standard—we can face that truth together knowing Christ loves you deeply. But we are going to help get you there."

The challenge for a truly gospel education is to keep the bar of the law high while building structures that come under weak students to lift them to the standard. There are many challenges to caring for weakness. Hiring aides and tutors to work with students with special needs is expensive. Teaching strategies that help struggling students are some of the most impressive superpowers of great teachers—they only come with much experience. And there will be times that schools have to say, "We just don't have the resources to help you—I'm sorry." But a gospel school will never be content with "Our school is for the smart and studious." Gospel education must be formed in a way that any of God's children (who are willing and want it) can come and be formed in the love of Jesus.

So God uses both the law and the gospel in the formation of these young lives. If the law is a chisel for cutting out the marble, the gospel is the breath that makes the marble statue come alive. These children are living works of art. The school is a workshop; Jesus is the Great Artist making them in his own image. Legalist and Lawless may be just cultural moods that try to distort the Artist's work—but Love is a real person who knows his material well (each child is a unique slab of marble). Like all good workshops, his is well-ordered for his craft of forming humans in love. And the orderliness of his workshop is the topic of our next chapter.

And the more I considered Christianity, the more I found that while it had established a rule and order, the chief aim of that order was to give room for good things to run wild.

G. K. Chesterton, *Orthodoxy*

3

THE LITURGY OF THE DAY

In the 1930s, part of Dietrich Bonhoeffer's resistance against the Nazis was to found an underground seminary whose communal life was structured around spiritual disciplines. He wrote a book on the culture of this community, *Life Together*, which has been a classic among Christians ever since.

I recently re-read my well-worn copy of *Life Together* and was surprised to find one chapter with no markings in it. I've read the book many times, so every chapter had important quotes underlined with stars next to them—except one, titled "The Day Together." As I read the chapter, I realized there were no markings because I'd never lived in a communal setting like the one Bonhoeffer was describing. I'd never shared the kind of life with other Christians in which our whole day was structured around devotion to God. I just couldn't relate.

But on this more recent read, it dawned on me that the community Bonhoeffer was describing is very similar to the community our children enjoy at school. Just about everything he described in that chapter—Bible reading, prayer, meals, work—all provide a daily spiritual rhythm to our school community as well.

Bonhoeffer's illegal, clandestine seminary at Finkenwalde, developed in the hostile world of Nazi Germany, can provide a model for us today. Schools have the unique opportunity to give children precisely the kind of community Bonhoeffer had envisioned, in a world that (in perhaps less dramatic fashion) is also turning away from God.

In the previous chapter, we considered how only the gospel can change the heart of a child. The new heart is a gift of grace, and obedience flows from it. Gospel change is inside-out, and school rules must reflect that truth.

But Christians have also noted that change happens outside-in as well. As a heart is inwardly turned toward God, it must be shaped outwardly by the community to become more like its King. The apostle Paul compared this discipleship process to being in labor in order to bear spiritual children (Gal 4:19). He longed for his children's hearts to be formed into the shape of Christ's inner life so that their emotions, dreams, thought patterns, griefs, desires, and everything else about them would come to be more like Jesus. How do our hearts get formed in love from the outside in? Paul also called his spiritual children to imitate him as he followed Jesus (1 Cor 11:1).

Theologians from Paul to Augustine to Aquinas to Lewis have taught that desires and affections are deeply shaped by our personal and shared habits. James K. A. Smith puts it this way:

> It is crucial for us to recognize that our ultimate loves, longings, desires, and cravings are learned. And because love is a habit, our hearts are calibrated through imitating exemplars and being immersed in practices that over time, index our hearts to a certain end.[1]

Historically, Christians have formed communities to immerse ourselves in just such practices. The Benedictine monastic tradition, for example, had a profound effect on European civilization over the thousand years following the fall of Rome, playing a key role in the development of Western education and social values.

When you hear that a school is like a monastery, you might think the goal is to barricade children from the world. It is true that monks left the decadence of the Roman world to pursue a life in service to God. But at their best, monasteries had a strong missionary purpose. They were devoted to hospitality, the education of common people, evangelism, works of mercy, and care for the poor. They were also industrious, making advances in agriculture, travel, and economics. It was the monasteries that brought the gospel into the barbarian world of Western Europe in the centuries following the fall of Rome. The spiritual discipline of the monks prepared them for a life of mission. In a similar way, as Western culture erodes in the United States, classical Christian schools—places of learning, love, and spiritual formation—have the potential to play a similar missionary role.

During the time of the sixteenth-century Reformation, John Calvin and other Reformers didn't reject the monastic vision of the medieval church but expanded it. Though he was critical of monastic vows, Calvin believed that a rhythmic, holy life formed around Christ and the Word of God was not just for monks and clergy but for all Christians. He envisioned his whole city being a monastery, with all the worship, work, and communal life done in harmony, all to the glory of God.[2]

How does all this inform classical Christian education? It shows us that everyday routines are essential for forming students in what they will love. God has appointed certain activities to form his people: the study of the Bible, prayer, fellowship, and eating together (Acts 2:42–47). God has intended for these spiritual disciplines—these habits—to happen in community. When done in community, they aren't burdensome but an experience of grace.

At our school, therefore, we've structured the students' day as a "liturgy." The word liturgy (*leitourgia* in Greek) means a "public work"—that is, an activity that a community gathers to do together so they can be formed toward a common purpose. Sunday worship is the main liturgy of the Christian life. And the rhythms of Bible reading, prayer, fellowship, and meals should spill over to create a kind of liturgy in the Christian home. The school day reflects a liturgy as well—an order of service that, when followed day by day for thirteen years, must have a profound influence in forming a young life.

So what are the liturgical elements that should fill the day of a classical school student? Our school's day includes the following elements, which largely overlap with Bonhoeffer's vision in *Life Together*.

SONG

The day begins with praise to God. As soon as their bags are settled, students grab their song books, assemble, and devote the day to God's glory with psalms, hymns, and spiritual songs (Col 3:16). Singing is of such paramount importance in a gospel-centered classical school that it will receive its own chapter later on.

PRAYER (ESPECIALLY THE PSALMS)

Once per week, these assembled times of song are lengthened to a full chapel service. The younger Grammar School students enter the sanctuary single file through a row of older Logic and Rhetoric students on either side, singing in harmony over them the enchanting words of the Sanctus: "Holy, holy, holy, Lord, God of power and might. Heaven and earth are full of your glory. Hosanna in the highest." On these days, not only do the students sing hymns, but the older students lead the rest of the school in prayer.

The Psalms are traditionally known as the prayer book of the Bible. God's people have used them to meditate on his truth and promises day and night (Ps 1:2). Meditating means not simply reading, but ruminating, dwelling on, and drawing out meaning and application for our lives. Bonhoeffer put special emphasis on the Psalms:

> Whenever the Psalter is abandoned, an incomparable treasure vanishes from the Christian church. With its recovery will come unsuspected power.[3]

To encourage meditation from the Psalms, each week a Logic or Rhetoric student is assigned a psalm to expand into a corporate prayer for the whole school. It's remarkable to hear the spiritual depth that comes from these young people.

CHAPEL LESSONS

These weekly chapel assemblies also include teaching. The chapel schedule is built around the primary texts used historically by Christians for discipleship. When our Lord told the apostles to make disciples by "teaching them to observe all that I have commanded" (Matt 28:20)—where should we look for the teaching that Jesus commanded? Well, the Gospel of Matthew is structured around five key sermons Jesus gave his disciples that lay out the basic teaching for Christian discipleship:

+ The Sermon on the Mount (Matt 5–7)
+ The Sermon on Mission (Matt 10)
+ The Parables of the Kingdom (Matt 13)
+ The Sermon on the Church (Matt 18)
+ The Olivet Discourse (Matt 23–25)[4]

Along with these sermons, our school uses the Ten Commandments, the Apostles' Creed, the Lord's Prayer, and Proverbs 1–9 (historically used by Jewish teachers for training adolescents). We draw on all these rich resources to create a rotating chapel schedule for both the Grammar School and the secondary school. These key texts are taught line by line, week by week, by local pastors in short chapel lessons. These lessons end up covering a wide variety of real-life topics from lust and sexuality to peer pressure, anger, and anxiety. Every student will study through each of these texts three times during his or her education, all the while laying a firm foundation in Christian doctrine, ethics, and spirituality.

SCRIPTURE MEDITATION

If there's one thing a Christian education should give a child, it's familiarity with the whole Bible—Old and New Testaments. After our students begin their day in song and prayer, they immediately go to their classrooms to take up their first order of business: reading, meditating on, and discussing the Word of God. These devotional times take about 15–30 minutes at the beginning of each day and train the students in the habit of starting their day with God's Word. Our hope is that, in adulthood, the Bible will never be intimidating but a comfort and joy to pick up and read as a part of their daily rhythm.

In first grade, our students read straight through Genesis and Matthew aloud, one chapter per day; in second grade, Exodus and Luke. Beginning in third grade, they read straight through the Pentateuch, historical books, wisdom literature, and much of the Prophets. The Old Testament is largely narrative and less conceptual than the letters of Paul (for example), which makes it ideal for Grammar School students to grasp.

Logic School students use this morning devotional time to read through the New Testament and discuss it. Rhetoric students read through the Bible twice over the course of four years. Our goal is that every student will read through the whole Bible at least three times during his or her education.

Such a systematic plan for reading the Bible also encourages teachers to be ever more proficient in discussing the section of the Bible their students read through each year. For example, if the fifth-grade teacher reads through the Minor Prophets with her students year after year, she will become more deeply versed in this section of the Bible.

It's also crucial at a gospel-centered classical school that teachers learn to talk about the Bible in a way that focuses on Jesus. Too often, our default seems to be to turn every story in the Bible into a moral lesson about good or bad behavior. But the main message of the Bible is about the Seed of the woman crushing the Serpent's head (Gen 3:15). Jesus said the whole Old Testament is about him (Luke 24:27). All the saints of the Old and New Testaments are sinners who have been saved by grace through faith in Jesus. Every prophet, priest, king, sacrifice, act of salvation, judge, temple, altar, and circumcision in the Old Testament is pointing to Jesus. Our children should grow up amazed that the hero of the Bible is not them, but Christ. So, every morning, when our students read the Scriptures, they conclude their discussion by asking, "How is this passage about Jesus?"

MEALS

In both the Rule of Benedict and Bonhoeffer's *Life Together*, meals play an important role in the life of the community. Their visions are different: in the monasteries, monks ate while someone read to them. (We often use lunch as a time for reading aloud to Grammar students.) But in Bonhoeffer's vision, mealtime is like a small holiday in the middle of our work. Lunch should have a festive quality. Students should look forward to it. In the midst of trading chips for pudding or playing outside, they will prove Bonhoeffer's words true: "Ever since Jesus Christ sat at table with his disciples, the table fellowship of his community has been blessed by his presence."[5]

The spiritual significance of meals comes from our Lord, who opened the kingdom to sinners by eating with them. The climax of Christian worship is a meal (the Lord's Supper) and the hope of eternal life is a meal (the marriage supper of the Lamb in Rev 19). And don't forget the playing: "And the streets of the city shall be full of boys and girls playing in its streets" (Zech 8:5).

WORK

One of the major differences between the Christian monastic tradition and the philosophical schools of the ancient world is that Christians have always believed work is good and pleasing to God. God himself worked six days in creating the world, after all. We reflect him in our work of creativity and fruitfulness.

The ancient world saw contemplation as leisure and physical labor as work. Work was reserved for the lower classes. Though education is often an experience of blissful contemplation, most children will find a classical education to be hard work, too. Though a school should respect the young frame of a child (Ps 103:13–14) and be reasonable in its expectations, it should still be demanding. The spiritual importance of work for children has two aspects in the daily life of a classical school: Students need to work, and they need to be physical.

Students need to work. A challenging classical education will demand hard work from students, it will stretch them, and it might even occasionally make them cry. This is because education in the Bible is described as discipline (*paideia*). As we saw earlier, education is an extension of healthy discipline God intends children to receive from their parents.

> We have had earthly fathers who disciplined us and we respected them. … For the moment all discipline seems painful rather than pleasant, but later it yields the peaceful fruit of righteousness to those who have been trained by it. (Heb 12:9, 11)

Learning to work through discomfort is an essential component of the spiritual formation of children, and they will only be formed this way through hard work. Such discipline is not in the least contrary to a formation in love. Love often looks like being able to suffer for a long period of time for the good of others. Discipline and suffering are generally important means through which God grows us in our love for him and others.

By emphasizing hard work, we see that education must encompass the whole person: spiritual and physical. Classical Christian educators Robert Littlejohn and Charles Evans put it this way:

> Clearly, reading is a work of both mind and body. Similarly, the mental discipline and focus required in athletics has implications for the discipline and mental focus required for academic study. Physical discipline produces self-control, while perseverance through difficult activities produces patience and creates habits of hard work in attaining goals—virtues that are as invaluable in the classroom as they are in an athletic event.[6]

So, then, students need not only to work but to be physical. The Christian emphasis on work is emphatically not a sole focus on the labors of the mind. Our Lord took on flesh. He worked with his hands as a carpenter and, therefore, dignified physical labor. It was the Greeks, not the Christians, who believed physical work was lesser in worth than the spiritual activity of the intellect.

The physicality of the daily liturgy includes recess. Students need to play. They need to run, chase, throw, kick, fall, and get up and do it all over again. Bonhoeffer loved to incorporate play into the disciplined life of Finkenwalde:

> Whatever they thought of the disciplines and the daily devotions, no one at Finkenwalde could complain that there was no fun. Most afternoons and evenings a time was set aside for hiking or sports. Bonhoeffer was forever organizing games, just as his mother had done in their family.[7]

The classical model of education has always recognized the importance of the gymnasium—or what we would call physical education. Classical schools today need to be careful to avoid an overemphasis on the mind over the body.

A NOTE ON UNIFORMS

You may not think of clothing as a part of the liturgical rhythm of a student's day, but uniforms similarly shape the character of the children in the community. (Monasteries, too, had rules about attire that helped cultivate humility in the brothers who lived there; it played a role in the spiritual discipline of the community.) Our school began with uniforms simply because other schools we respected followed this practice. But since then, parents and staff have all come to appreciate how important uniforms are to our culture. How does a simple and sensible uniform policy help form students? There are many ways, but here are a few:

+ Uniforms help students take on the proper mindset for school days: "I'm dressed for class. It's time to work."
+ They bring unity among students, minimizing visible signs of wealth or fashion or other social distinctions among them and their families, which can cause distraction, conflict, envy, or pride.
+ They encourage bodily propriety and modesty.
+ They make dress-down days a treat.

The habits of the school liturgy are subtle ways the school is structured to cultivate the heart and love of Jesus in the students. This kind of discipleship has the power to train a generation of missionaries whose hearts and minds have been shaped to glorify God and enjoy him in love.

The idea of Christianity and the meaning of reality belong together like lock and key: they make sense together.

Herman Bavinck, *Christian Worldview*

4

A CHRISTIAN WORLDVIEW

At this point, you might be wondering, "Okay, so far, we've talked about God's promises to our covenant children, what a gospel culture looks like in a classical Christian school, and the spiritual disciplines that form the hearts of students. But when are we going to start talking about *learning*? Isn't that what schools are for?"

Yes and no. A classical Christian school doesn't teach students to learn for the sake of learning. The school exists for formation in the image of Christ. Schools shape the hearts and minds of young people, equipping them to serve God in the world throughout their lives. So the emphasis we've placed on formation cannot be assumed or taken for granted. It is utterly foundational for discipling children well.

We're now ready, though, to begin to turn toward the subjects and methods of what we typically think of as the heart of education. But before we can fully make that turn, we need just one more chapter on education's intellectual foundation.

Whether we know it or not, every one of us brings foundational assumptions to our understanding of the world. These assumptions shape the way we approach everything, including learning and teaching. And these assumptions (whether Christian or not) are always built on faith.

Before becoming a pastor, I studied mathematics. I remember the class that formed my love for math—a rigorous third-year college course on proofs. In this class, we would build mathematics from the ground up and prove every assertion along the way. On the first day of that class, the professor handed us a sheet of paper with eight axioms that would be the starting point for all our work that quarter.

Axioms are unprovable assumptions upon which other knowledge must be built. For our math class, they were simple statements like "Any number times 1 gives you the same number." You might think that's obvious, but how do you know it's *always* true? It can't be proven. Or take the equation $a + b = b + a$. Do you always get the same sum on each side, no matter what? Well, yes. Again, you might think these equations seem obvious, but the important part is that they are both obvious and unprovable. You must assume them in order to do math in the first place. You must take them on faith. Even in mathematics, faith comes before reason.

This is true of everything we learn. Every field of knowledge is loaded with assumptions from the start. History considers some events more important than others. Based on what? Science assumes nature has always acted in repeatable, predictable ways, according to unchanging laws. This may seem obvious to modern people, but that doesn't make it true or false.

In a Christian school, the foundational axioms that support all of our knowledge are the basic doctrines of the Christian faith taught in the Bible, most briefly summarized in the Apostles' Creed. These doctrines provide the key information for a truly Christian education:

+ This is our Father's world
+ His Son Jesus has been given all authority in heaven and earth as the true King over creation
+ The Holy Spirit directs all of human history according to God's purposes
+ The Bible is God's special revelation of himself to humanity
+ Humanity is fallen and our only hope of redemption is in Christ
+ God will put everything right and make all things new

Though there is much historical evidence for the veracity of Christianity, ultimately, the truth of these statements cannot be proven without a foundation of faith. In fact, these statements are how we test the truth of other claims. The Bible and the Christian faith form the basis of a beautiful worldview and the intellectual foundation for a lifetime of learning about God, his world, and ourselves. As C. S. Lewis famously put it, "I believe in Christianity as I believe that the sun has risen: not only because I see it, but because by it I see everything else."[1]

The Christian faith not only explains our spiritual life, but it illumines everything about God, his world, and humanity rightly. If you think of the world as blurry to our fallen minds, the Christian faith is like glasses that bring everything into clarity.

We call these lenses for seeing clearly a Christian worldview. There is no area of life or knowledge left untouched by the Christian worldview. It's an amazingly coherent and comprehensive framework for understanding God, his world, and humanity. And throughout history, this worldview has proven to be immensely fruitful in improving human culture.

The cultural development surrounding the movement of the gospel is profound. Much of the world as we know it—whether political and economic theories, the practice of universal education, modern science and medicine, the development of human rights, the rejection of slavery, and the list goes on and on—is the direct fruit of the gospel's influence.[2] Our children must learn to understand history through the lens of the gospel. Studying Western civilization matters to us not because it's Eurocentric but because it's where the roots of the gospel happen to have grown most deeply into the soil of human culture (at least so far). We must remember, too, that the Christian foundations of Western civilization don't belong simply to the West: For the first thousand years of the church, Christianity was more prominent in the East and in northern Africa.

So why shouldn't we be surprised when historians believe certain events in history are more important that others? The Bible tells us that the main storyline of human history is about the Seed of the woman crushing the Serpent's head (Gen 3:15). This is the story of Christ bringing redemption to all the places affected by the Evil One—that is, all nations. The history of each nation matters to God, but he gives special attention to the progress of the gospel. The key thread to history (as you can see in the history recorded in the Bible) is the promises of God in Christ that passed from Abraham to Israel, to Babylon and Persia, to Greece and Rome, to Asia Minor in the early church, to Syria and North Africa in the time of the church fathers, to Europe in the Middle Ages, to the UK and the Americas in the modern era, and to Asia, South America, and Africa in our own age.

Or why shouldn't we be surprised when modern people believe science is a reliable source of knowledge? We believe in a rational God who rules nature according to providence. He is wise, and so he rules in an orderly manner. As the Lord of nature, he, of course, has power to make exceptions to the laws of nature by doing what we call miracles. But the laws of nature and miracles are both instances of how the Almighty rules the universe according to his will. God gave us senses to observe the natural world. "The hearing ear and the seeing eye, the LORD has made them both" (Prov 20:12). But Christians believe that by studying the patterns of the natural world, we are learning not about the accidents of blind chance but about the wisdom of our creative and good God. I could say something similar about studying literature, art, music, philosophy, or language.

Unfortunately, many of us in the church have failed to give our children a robust Christian worldview. The hard truth is, we often don't have a robust Christian worldview to pass on to them. How have we fallen short? I'd like to offer two reasons: We tend to either separate our faith from the rest of life or let pride infect and undermine our doctrine.

First, we tend to separate our faith from the rest of life. Especially over the past century, the majority of North American Christians have entrusted the formation of their children to government schools—with disastrous results. Now, this isn't simply a matter of Christian parental neglect. People sometimes don't have much choice; private schools can feel like a luxury reserved for the upper middle class, if one exists in a family's area at all. Or a family may have a child with disabilities that a public school is usually far more equipped to accommodate than many under-resourced Christian schools. These are serious concerns, which is why I think many more churches need to get in the business of starting schools (or homeschool co-ops) that are accessible to as many families as possible. Most congregations have whole education wings sitting empty and unused all week. Fill them with the children of your church! Fill them with your neighbors' children, too!

But money and accessibility aren't the only concerns at play. We greatly underestimate the indoctrination that takes place in any school, public or private, Christian or otherwise. Education is never neutral. Remember axioms, the unproven statements on which we build our knowledge? Human beings are always working from non-negotiable commitments, which means we always have a worldview. Often, the most dogmatic and intolerant worldviews are present in places that say, "We have no religious agenda; we're neutral." An unspoken worldview is very difficult to protect your kids against.

North American government schools can be some of the most dogmatically "neutral" places on earth. As a result, many Christian children grow up for seventeen years immersed in a godless learning environment for *thirty hours* per week. In all those thousands of hours, the name of God will never be spoken with reverence. Not only that, but many unbiblical views will be proclaimed as undisputed truth.

What's the effect of such an environment on young faith? How is a heart formed in a school liturgy (every school has one) that doesn't submit to God? It's no wonder Christianity has been in steep decline among young people. Something is seriously broken in the passing on of Christianity to the next generation.

A hundred years ago, people would say they didn't believe in historic Christianity because science had disproved the possibility of miracles. But those people would still go to church. They thought religion was still important for learning morals. Increasingly, the present generation sees the God of the Bible as immoral and the church as oppressive. This view of the Christian faith is assumed and reinforced in many government schools today.

If we Christians continue to think education is neutral, or relegate our faith to the realm of private spirituality, we will also continue to see the faith of our children decimated by a culture now openly hostile to historic Christianity.

But separating faith from the rest of life isn't the only reason we may struggle with a less-than-robust Christian worldview. We can also allow pride to undermine our doctrine.

It's a very human reaction to become proud in the midst of hostility, like the brainy kid bullied on the playground who goes home to ruminate on his intellectual superiority. Conservative Christians act this way all the time. We think, "We have the truth. We have a superior worldview. The world might try to bully us, but they're a bunch of wicked idiots. We just need to believe the right things, keep on the straight and narrow, and we'll take back cultural control from the crazies." Such thinking blinds Christians to our own shortcomings, ignorance, and especially sin. How many fundamentalists growing up in such a self-assured environment have been utterly blindsided by the intellectual complexity of the real world when they got to college? "Before destruction a man's heart is haughty" (Prov 18:12). Spiritual pride is always a temptation for Christians, maybe more so within the classical Christian school movement.

Thoughtful, committed Christians are particularly prone to trust in our own understanding and to miss what really has the power to change things. Sociologist James Davison Hunter has written about the ambitions of the Religious Right, which thought that, by giving Americans a Christian worldview, they could transform the culture. It turns out that, over the course of forty years, that project has largely failed. A quarter of Americans identify as evangelical or born-again Christians, but evangelical cultural influence in academia, media, entertainment, and politics is (comparatively) dismal.[3]

Why the disconnect? The truth is, people rarely act on the basis of a rational worldview. We act from what we most truly love and worship. That's why this chapter on worldview must come after the chapters on gospel culture and the formative liturgy that shapes a child's desires. Worldview flows from worship.

Worldview talk can make us proud, thinking we are the masters of true knowledge while looking down on the foolish and sinful masses. But worshipping the true God should transform our lives and make us humble. It should make us realize we are the fools who need to be instructed—the sinners who need to be forgiven. The fully Christian mind is both shaped by the truth and steeped in humility. "Be not wise in your own eyes" (Prov 3:7). "If anyone imagines that he knows something, he does not yet know as he ought to know" (1 Cor 8:2). This truth is vital for classical schools if we're going to be places committed to forming children in love. Pride not only stifles knowledge; it poisons love.

So how, then, can a school train children to have their whole lives shaped by Christ without training them in pride?

At our school, we uphold four key principles for a humble yet bold Christian worldview:

1. *Our worldview is the gospel.* Pride comes when we think the sinners are "out there" in the world. The gospel destroys such arrogance. "For if anyone thinks he is something, when he is nothing, he deceives himself" (Gal 6:3). Christians confess that we're lost, ignorant, and blind by nature. And though Jesus receives us with loving arms, remaining sin affects our behavior and even our thinking until we finally go to be with him in glory. We cannot be informed into heaven; we need to be saved. When the gospel is at the center of our worldview, we avoid the error of pride in our approach to education.

2. *Our worldview is the Bible.* The Bible speaks to all of life. If you read through the Bible, you will find it addresses all the important themes of human life: God, nature, family, friendship, forgiveness, politics, money, literature, work, sex. No sphere of life is left untouched by the light of God's holy word or left unshaped by his counsel. When God's word is at the center of education, we avoid the error of compartmentalizing our faith.

3. *Our worldview is a tradition.* One of the great antidotes to pride is tradition. It's rare—but so good!—when a young person says, "Those older than me probably know better than I do. I need to stop talking and listen to them." Students need not only living elders but also those long dead. The apostle Paul said to "stand firm and hold to the traditions that you were taught by us" (2 Thess 2:15).

One major reason Christians have lost cultural influence is because we've ignored our theological heritage. Imagine a young medical student who said he didn't need the medical tradition to become a doctor: "Just give me a scalpel and a cadaver and I'll figure this out on my own." You wouldn't let that proud doctor anywhere near your body. This is what the American church has largely done. We have a millennia-long tradition of a worldview that has built whole civilizations. Yet we have neglected this tradition to our peril. The heart of classical education is about passing this tradition down to the next generation. G. K. Chesterton once said,

> It ought to be the oldest things that are taught to the youngest people; the assured and experienced truths that are put first to the baby. But in a school today the baby has to submit to a system that is younger than himself. The flopping infant of four actually has more experience, and has weathered the world longer, than the dogma to which he is made to submit.[4]

In our school, we tell parents that their children will be indoctrinated in the Reformed theology of the Westminster Confession and Catechisms.[5] These standards are rooted in the rule of faith, structured around the Apostles' Creed, the Ten Commandments, and the Lord's Prayer. Children memorize the catechism and adolescents debate the confession. Even for families in churches that aren't Reformed or Presbyterian, we believe their children are better served by a deep dive into theology within one tradition than by a shallow swim in no particular tradition in an effort to accommodate them all.

4. *Our worldview is a person.* The crucial protection against both compartmentalization and pride is the person of Jesus. If we aren't mastering the truth but being mastered by the truth, then who is the Master? Before his feet, we learn not to think of ourselves more highly than we ought. There, we learn not

to be wise in our own eyes. In that humble place, we also learn that he is the solution to all the world's riddles. Everything holds together in him (Col 1:17). The answer to every riddle is not a doctrine but a person: the God-man.

When God's covenant has created a gospel culture in a school, built around a daily liturgy that forms children in love and trains them in a Christian worldview centered on Jesus Christ by faith, only then are we ready to talk about classical learning. This is because classical learning shouldn't be an add-on to the gospel, as if we could move on from Christ to talk about a style of education. No, Christians have found throughout history that classical education is the natural outflow of a Christ-centered education. When educators approach schooling from the standpoint of the gospel, that education tends to take on a classical form. So, in the pages that follow, we're not moving on from the gospel. We're showing how the gospel gives shape to a classical liberal arts education.

Nearly all wisdom we possess, that is to say,
true and sound wisdom, consists of two parts:
the knowledge of God and of ourselves.

John Calvin, *Institutes of the Christian Religion*

5

TRAINING IN WISDOM

We turn now from the foundational importance of the gospel to the pedagogical strategy of the school: classical education.

You may feel that much of what we've explored so far has been familiar territory: the gospel, the Bible, prayer, praise, and the Christian worldview. But as we move into the second half of the book, the land might begin to feel more foreign, described with words like dialectic and rhetoric. Don't be intimidated. These words are simply shorthand for the ways Christians have applied the gospel to education throughout history. As we focus on classical education, *we're not moving on from the gospel,* but showing now how the gospel shapes the intellectual life of a Christian school.

So what is classical education? There have been many attempts to define it: Is it an education in the great books of the Western canon? Is it a three-stage process of learning built around the Trivium—that is, grammar, logic, and rhetoric? Is it teaching Latin and Greek? Is it an emphasis on speech and debate or the skills of thinking and communicating well?

All these elements are part of the picture, and I'll discuss them in the pages to come. Most specifically, however, classical education is a long-proven training method by which God forms young people in the wisdom of Christ. The supremely wise person, after all, is Jesus, in whom "all the treasures of wisdom and knowledge" are hidden (Col 2:3). So maybe the simplest way to define classical education is *training in wisdom.*

Let's focus on wisdom first.

WISDOM IS INTEGRATED KNOWLEDGE AND FRUITFUL SKILL

Cornelius Plantinga Jr. has defined wisdom as "a knowledge of God's world and a knack for fitting oneself into it."[1] Wisdom is both knowledge and knack (another word for knack is skill). Wisdom is the way the Bible describes a person well suited to live and love and work in the world God has made. Drawing on the book of Proverbs and Plantinga's definition, we'll define wisdom in these two ways:

> Wisdom is an integrated knowledge of God, his world, and oneself.[2]
>
> Wisdom is the fruitful skill of living in goodness, beauty, and truth.

Take a moment to reflect on each of these definitions. Each word is carefully chosen. For a classical education to be successful, it must be structured to give a student these two things: knowledge and skill. In the first half of this chapter, we'll explain more about these two parts of wisdom. In the second half, we'll explain how a classical education trains students in wisdom.

1. *Wisdom is integrated knowledge.* An emphasis on integrated knowledge means that classical education strives to tie together the many parts of learning that often get separated: literature, history, Bible, science, math, writing, and so on. An integrated education resists the fracturing of knowledge into separate subjects, constantly striving to discern how the various things we learn fit into a consistent whole. Colossians tells us that "in [Christ] all things hold together" (Col 1:17). The wise person recognizes how everything is connected in Jesus.

To get a sense of why this is important, it might help to draw a contrast with the modern educational system. There are deep inconsistencies between (for example) the humanities and the sciences. Humanities departments tend to be relativistic—everyone has his or her own truth and reality, each valid as long as it doesn't harm others. The science departments, meanwhile, are rationalistic—nothing is true unless verified by impartial experimental testing. One says there is no single truth for everyone; the other says there is but severely restricts that truth's character. Who's right?[3]

Such an education is fractured. No wonder so many modern people feel anxious and aimless about the purpose of our lives! If we've never been taught to see any unity within the world's complexity, how can we ever expect to experience true wholeness? The way we've been taught to see the world is incoherent.

In contrast, training in Christian wisdom brings wholeness and coherence to the soul by integrating all the areas of learning in Christ himself, who is the Creator, Redeemer, and Lord of all things. How are the humanities and sciences reconciled in him? He is the Lawgiver behind the laws of nature; he is the Author of the story of history; he is the Artist who invented color, form, and subtlety; he is the Goodness at the heart of morality; he is the Hero of the Bible; he is the Word from whom language is derived; he dwells in the triune community of which human society is a reflection. Life makes sense in Jesus.

When we acknowledge Christ as the center of education, it opens the path toward integrating all the subjects in him. Not only do we start to see everything connected to him, but also we expect to find all things connected to each other in both predictable and surprising ways. We see how math is deeply tied to history. Euclid transformed the Greco-Roman world, just as Newton transformed the modern world. Literature interacts with theology, and theology shapes political theory. Latin is the language of the sciences. Because Christ is Lord of history and the Creator of nature, through each of these subjects, students are being trained in his wisdom. We could never make all these connections in our own minds, but all things come from his, and "we have the mind of Christ" (1 Cor 2:16). Our learning isn't the result of our wisdom but is his wisdom shared with us. And we will never run out of things to learn from him.

C. S. Lewis was a paragon of this kind of integrated learning. Whether he was writing children's stories, popular theology, medieval literary criticism, or science fiction, the same vision of the world came through. He had a "single-mindedness" that his close friend Owen Barfield described this way: "Somehow what he thought about everything was secretly present in what he said about anything."[4] No matter the subject, Lewis's Christ-centered vision of the universe came through. This is the kind of mind we hope to form in a classical school. Not only is everything the student knows profoundly connected, but at the center of all knowledge stands the good, beautiful, and true Son of God.

How does this relate to our thesis that education should be a training in love? Love binds things together, especially things that are distinct. When love shapes a marriage, a man and woman fit together by God's design. When love shapes knowledge, likewise, we find a beautiful marriage between math and medieval history, Moses and maps of Mauritania. Since Christ is the one whose love holds all things together, we should not be surprised to find a beautiful harmony between the sciences and the humanities.

This wholeness and love at the heart of an integrated education brings sanity to a young life—something desperately needed in our culture. The fractured modern worldview has elevated yet isolated the individual, draining the universe of coherent meaning. This has resulted in chronic anxiety, especially among young people.[5] We have forgotten that the same God who orders nature orders human societies and human souls. Classical Christian education gives wholeness to our sense of being in the world. In doing so, it gives wisdom. The wise survey God's world and see that "in him we live and move and have our being" (Acts 17:28). They sense how everything holds together in a harmony of goodness, beauty, and truth.

As that harmony becomes known, such wisdom doesn't just stay in students' head. It translates into skills.

That brings me to my second definition of wisdom:

2. *Wisdom is fruitful skill.* In the Bible, wisdom is never simply knowledge. True knowledge is always fruitful—that is, effective and productive for multiplying truth, goodness, and beauty. Wisdom is also never simply skill. Skill in practicing unrighteousness or selfishness can never count as wisdom, because it can't bear good fruit. Wise people in the Bible are artists, church planters, and administratively minded kings.

They write just laws, run productive households, and build successful businesses. Wisdom is a culture-making power. It creates things for the good of others and leaves the world changed for the better.

Skill in our work is a matter of character and a key component to a fruitful Christian life. In fact, doing our work well may be the primary way we will love our neighbors as ourselves throughout our lives. How many Christians consider competence in our calling to be a part of our sanctification in Christ?

In both the book of Proverbs and in classical education, perhaps the most important wise skill we can cultivate in ourselves and in others is our use of words. The Bible teaches that God's creativity comes through his speaking (John 1:1), and humans similarly rule the world largely through our words (Gen 2:19). Salvation comes through speaking as well, as ministers proclaim the Word of God (Rom 10:17). We should not see speaking as an alternative to fruitfulness—as empty talk (1 John 3:16–18). Rather, we should treat our words as an essential way in which we are called to love our neighbors throughout our lives. Our lips and hands work together in the pursuit of goodness, beauty, and truth. "From the fruit of his mouth a man is satisfied with good, and the work of a man's hand comes back to him" (Prov 12:14).

Those who can speak goodness, beauty, and truth are those who shape the world into greater wholeness. Good leadership is largely speaking the right things at the right time and in the right way. Those who lead well are those who tell us the true story of the world, and call us to play our part in it. "Do you see a man skillful in his work?" Proverbs 22:29 asks. "He will stand before kings; he will not stand before obscure men."

Learning that kind of skill never happens haphazardly. Fruitful skills are a gift of God's grace, but they are stewarded through hard work, discipline, orderliness, conscientiousness, and careful intentionality. "The hand of the diligent will rule, while the slothful will be put to forced labor" (Prov 12:24). For a school to be effective in training wise leaders, we must be diligent in cultivating both the knowledge and skill that belong to godly wisdom.

And as soon as we hear this, we must remember that the great leader—the one who loves with his words and work—is Jesus himself. "As the branch cannot bear fruit by itself, unless it abides in the vine, neither can you, unless you abide in me" (John 15:4). His Spirit must produce fruit in us. He is the Storyteller. He is the Wisdom of God. No wonder Jesus says, "Apart from me you can do nothing" (John 15:5)!

THE SHAPE OF WISE TRAINING

In a classical Christian school, we want to train young people to have an integrated understanding of God, his world, and themselves and the skills to communicate goodness, beauty, and truth. We believe if we can do that, we have set them up for a lifetime of learning and productive service to God in their homes, churches, and callings. We've explored how classical education is a pedagogical method focused on wisdom; now, let's look at its method directly—how it is, as defined above, a *training* in wisdom. There are again two key aspects of a classical approach: the teacher and what is taught.

1. *For integrated knowledge, cultivate teachers who are a living curriculum.* The integrating of knowledge can only happen in a person. Ultimately, that person is Jesus. He makes this complex world a sensible whole. But the teacher stands in the classroom as a representative of Christ—as someone in whom, in a reflected way, all things have begun to hold together like they do in him.

She must be a living curriculum: a book filled with timeless words, ideas, and stories but one that's always timely—always growing and maturing. Every year, her classes are improving, even without changing the scope and sequence of the assignments. Over the years, the language in this human-book gets stronger, the imagery more vivid, the wisdom more nuanced. Her suffering has kept the stories from being trite. The Author is constantly adding more pages that not only add to the previous story but often cast them in a new light.

Ask this book a question, and watch it open immediately to the relevant page and ask you one back. This book can read its students better than they can read it and offer its wisdom in a way suited to each. What a magical book!

Our Head of School, Diana Lim, likes to say that our teachers must embrace a personal pursuit of knowledge that leads to a "well-stocked" mind. The great nineteenth-century English preacher Charles Spurgeon said something similar about his students' need for broad and regular study:

> Store your minds very richly, and then, like merchants with crowded warehouses, you will have goods ready for your customers, and having arranged your good things upon the shelves of your mind, you will be able to hand them down at any time without the laborious process of going to market, sorting, folding, and preparing. ... Take it as a rule without exception, that to be able to overflow spontaneously you must be full.[6]

There is a temptation in the modern world to think we don't need broad learning because so much knowledge is at our fingertips on the internet. But that is not how wise people live. Can you imagine having a conversation about foreign policy, and every time a word like "tariff" or "sanction" came up, you had to go ask Google what they meant? It wouldn't happen. You would just avoid the conversation all together. We don't have conversations about things we know nothing about.

For this reason, the classical teacher loves learning and is constantly doing it—about anything that interests her. She loves the Scriptures. She loves books and talking about books. She loves going deep in her areas of instruction, and she loves finding connections to areas outside her specialty. She loves discussion and deep topics—such conversations are her greatest source of pleasure. She loves the practical and the impractical, the serious and the playful. Above all, she worships the one in whom all things hold together, and so, all things have begun to come together in her mind and heart as well.

The key word here is love. She loves everything about God and his good green world and loves exploring the mysteries of that world. As pastor George Grant has said, a teacher's goal is to "love the things you love in front of the people you love."[7]

If you're a teacher, know this: *Such a beautiful vision will crush you* unless and until all your love comes from being loved. Until you delight because you're delighted in. Until you are able to integrate because you've been made whole. "We love because he first loved us" (1 John 4:19). Don't forget that the gospel truths of the first half of this book apply to you as much as to your students.

Classical schools are truly great when every classroom has a wise living curriculum present who loves her particular subject and is loved by her ultimate Subject. The pupil rarely goes beyond his master. Christians rarely mature beyond their church leaders. So, teachers set the standard for the kind of humans that will be formed in the school.

2. *For skills in goodness, beauty, and truth, practice the seven liberal arts.* A school should focus on doing a few things really

well. Government schools have gradually been widening the scope of their role in a child's life. This could be understandable (if, for example, they are responding to neglect in the home). But the broader an education is conceived, the shallower the quality of learning in each area.

Historically, the Christian strategy for shaping young people in wisdom has focused on the seven liberal arts. These arts are divided into two classes: the Trivium (grammar, logic, and rhetoric) and the Quadrivium (arithmetic, geometry, astronomy, and music). The Trivium focuses on language skills and the Quadrivium mathematical skills. I believe a return to these fundamental arts is essential for a renewal in modern learning.

In the rest of this book, I'll explain how these liberal arts function in a modern gospel-centered school to cultivate goodness, beauty, and truth. But let's end this chapter on training in wisdom with a brief introduction to the method of that training.

The arts are called "liberal" because they are meant to train citizens in being free people (*liber* means "free" in Latin). In the modern world, we think that being free means I can follow my own passions, chasing whatever my heart demands. Freedom means nothing determining my path or standing in my way.

But the ancient world saw free people as those who could govern themselves. Because they were trained in virtue, they didn't need a tyrant to keep their passions in check. Their own self-discipline was sufficient. Hence, in an ironic way, there is empowerment found in submission to an order—to a tradition.[8]

The liberal arts are meant to empower students by training them in the classical subjects and methods best suited to cultivating people who are truly free: wise and godly men and women. As they read and discuss the great thinkers throughout history who have built civilizations, they join the Great

Conversation of the Western world and ask for themselves the deep questions of life, death, God, justice, and human society. In the next three chapters, we'll see how the Trivium gives children the cultural knowledge to join the Great Conversation of Western civilization, the logical precision to discern truth from error, and the grace to speak and write with subtlety, conviction, and persuasiveness. After that, we'll give two chapters to math, science, and music in which we'll see how the Quadrivium trains children in the orderly beauty of God's creation.

Classical education is an ancient practice. But there have also been some helpful contemporary innovations building on traditional conceptions of the liberal arts. In 1948, the playwright Dorothy Sayers presented a lecture at Oxford, "The Lost Tools of Learning." She called for a recovery of the Trivium in modern education, arguing that the Trivium was specially suited to the stages of a child's intellectual development. Each stage of learning should have a particular emphasis:

+ Grammar (3rd–6th grade): memorization of facts
+ Logic (7th–8th grade): formal reasoning and dialectical discussion
+ Rhetoric (9th–12th grade): effective speaking and writing

According to Sayers, every subject has its own grammar, logic, and rhetoric. But every student begins with grammar (dates, places, names, capitals, battles, parts of speech, animal species, poems, math facts, and so on). Through chants and songs, a wealth of facts can be absorbed efficiently by an elementary school student. Once he hits (roughly) seventh grade, however, he wants to start debating what he's learned—it's time for training in logic (especially since he's going to find himself committing all kinds of fallacies!). The high school years then polish the crude argument of the middle schooler into the persuasive and poetic speech of the rhetorician.

Over the last generation, classical schools have employed Sayers's insights—to great effect!—but have now built on and moved beyond her essay.[9] Limiting the Trivium to successive or developmental stages of learning can be overly rigid; it doesn't fully represent how Christians have historically understood the Trivium. Though the progress of the Trivium correlates broadly to a child's development, it's better to recognize that every stage of learning includes grammar, logic, and rhetoric.

We might think of these stages of learning like the related biblical categories of *knowledge* (grammar), *understanding* (logic), and *wisdom* (rhetoric).

> By *wisdom* a house is built,
> and by *understanding* it is established;
> By *knowledge* the rooms are filled
> with all precious and pleasant riches. (Prov 24:3–4, emphasis mine)

Kindergarteners need to learn the confidence to stand up to speak in front of adults and one another (rhetoric), while high schoolers will always have to learn new facts in the subjects they're studying (grammar). All learning happens this way, even for adults.

These arts are truly powerful, but a gospel education is always going to qualify how we speak about that power. Humans will always suffer when they are under the tyrannical rule of a sinful man, but self-governance is actually me just living under the rule of another sinful man—me! True liberal education is one that leads me to live under the rule of the one who promised us, "The truth will set you free" (John 8:32). To live in truth, goodness, and beauty means really to live in the true, good, and beautiful One who is Christ. Slavery to Christ is freedom; freedom of my own desires is actually another form of slavery. True self-control is a fruit of the Holy Spirit, the formation of the mind of Christ in me as a gift of grace. Education truly sets us free only when it leads us to him—the one who has loved us, not because of our wisdom but because of his goodness. And so, every step of the way, gospel education is about him. If everything holds together in Jesus, so too must the liberal arts.

The greatest service we can do to education today is to teach fewer subjects. No one has time to do more than a very few things well before he is twenty, and when we force a boy to be a mediocrity in a dozen subjects we destroy his standards, perhaps for life.

C. S. Lewis, *Surprised by Joy*

6

GRAMMAR

I would not object to someone calling the Grammar School a School of Magic. In the first years of school, a child learns the most basic magic powers of being human: reading, writing, and memorizing. Those three powers are basically the substance of grades K–6.

Most people don't think of these as magic powers. That's only because literacy is so commonplace. But this magic was not always so ubiquitous as it is today.[1]

Think about it. Ideas are spiritual realities; they have no physical substance. Yet they're mysteriously captured in language and stained into the pages of a book with ink. The book holds the idea (in some cases, for centuries) until it's unlocked by only the right wizarding powers. A *reader* is the special order of wizard able to unlock the book. The ideas, now free, flow out of the paper into the body of the reader, taking up residence in him. The ideas live in the reader like they did in the book but with one important difference: in the book, the ideas remained the same, like they were sleeping. When they take up residence in the reader, they become like seeds planted in fertile soil. The reader's own soul waters them while they grow and take shape. The new, larger ideas can then be transplanted into other books (this kind of wizard is called a *writer*) until another reader comes to germinate them.

Science alone can't explain this. I know photons bounce from the page of the book into the eye of the reader, but more than photons pass from the page to the eye—the spiritual idea in some sense rides on the back of the photon. How else does the idea get from the book to the soul? Can you see an idea or a soul under a microscope? It's not well explained without saying something magical—or rather, it's less explained than marveled at.

This is the magic that enables cities to be built, airplanes to be engineered, and governments to lead vast civilizations. Since we believe in a God who speaks, writes history, remembers his promises, and listens to the prayers of his people, Christians esteem every proper cultivation of these God-given capacities. We are worded beings—created and shaped by words—and we too shape the world with words. This magic flows from the image of God, and its overflow can be imparted even to a child. After just a few years of training, he or she can exercise these powers almost effortlessly. Yet this magic took centuries to develop, and some people groups still haven't learned it. (This doesn't diminish their dignity as image-bearers—they still have all the magical capacities that anyone else does.) In fact, most humans didn't know how to perform the magic of reading and writing until Christians began to teach it to the small and the great alike.

The first stage of a classical education is a training in this magic. It's called the Grammar School, granting children the awe-inspiring powers of reading, memorization, and writing.

READING

Historically, the subject of grammar has been variously defined: as simply learning to read and write (the *grammatike* of Plato and Aristotle), or "knowledge of what is normally said by poets and prose writers" (Dionysius Thrax), or more broadly, the knowledge needed for interpreting a text, including familiarity with history and geography (Quintilian).[2] Whether considered narrowly or broadly, a common theme among the ancients is that the first thing a child needs to learn in school is to read.

In fact, reading is the first thing humanity needs to learn in order to live in God's world. While individuals can observe nature or hear and believe the gospel even if illiterate, God has revealed himself explicitly to humanity as a whole *in a book*. We can only know God from reading or being read to. And from the earliest books of the Bible, it's clear that God intends for his people to be able to read his Word and understand it (Deut 6). Other historic cultures had wisdom books, but they were meant for kings and rulers. Reading was for the rich. But Proverbs was written for farmers and shepherds, too, because all of God's people need wisdom.

This is why missionaries the world over have started schools alongside churches. Monasteries taught barbarians to read; Reformers taught peasants to read. Learning to read has always been essential for discipleship, which is why Christians have been by far the greatest champions of universal literacy throughout history.

Gospel classical schools must excel at teaching students to read well, infusing a deep love of reading from the earliest ages. We start with the reliable methods of phonics in kindergarten and first grade. All year, at every level, reading is assigned every day. Typically, the more pages, the better. It's best that the reading is varied. Rotate short and long books, breezy and thick. Provide fun reads the kids naturally enjoy and others that stretch and shape their literary tastes. Of course, read God's Word. Read poems. Read science. But read, read, read.

St. Augustine, in *On Christian Teaching*, said there are basically two goals for education: learning to read the Bible and learning to tell others about it.[3] You might think that seems unbearably narrow as a scope for a contemporary education, but it's remarkable how expansive such a vision actually is when you reflect on it. To read the Bible well, it's not enough simply to be able to follow the words. A phonics-proficient seven-year-old will still struggle through Isaiah. Bible reading also demands knowledge of geography (Where is Jerusalem? Ethiopia?), an understanding of history (When were the Babylonian and Roman Empires?), and the basics of theology (What is atonement?). Augustine even says you need to know your math, since the Bible is full of numbers and numeric patterns! True literacy demands a richer cultural and experiential knowledge than the bare ABCs.

Though learning to decode words is essential, reading well is far more complex than simply being able to sound out words. That point was emphasized by English professor E. D. Hirsch, Jr. He studied the use of short-term memory during reading. Our brains must hold the beginning of each sentence in place while our eyes are making our way to the end. If the cultural context of any sentence in a book or newspaper article isn't quickly accessible to the brain of the reader, however, comprehension is nearly impossible. Hirsch calls these contexts necessary for comprehension "schemata":

> The reader is not just passively receiving meaning but is actively selecting the most appropriate schemata for making sense of the incoming words. Then the reader actively adjusts

> those schemata to the incoming words until a good fit is achieved. This process can work efficiently only if the reader has quick access to appropriate schemata. When the appropriate schemata are not quickly available, and the reader is forced to do a lot of pondering to construct them at the time of reading, the limits of short-term memory are quickly reached, and the process has to be painfully restarted.[4]

In cultures throughout the world, it has been basic wisdom that children need to memorize the fundamental elements of their cultural tradition if they're going to know how to live in that culture. The classical Grammar School teaches literacy not only by training in phonics but richly supplying the minds of children with the *cultural* grammar that supports their *linguistic* grammar.

How are these tools for reading transferred to a child? How do students gain this cultural literacy so vital for being able to read well? This brings us to the second magic power taught in the Grammar School.

MEMORIZING

Because literacy requires far more than phonics, Dorothy Sayers broadened the Grammar School to encompass not only learning to read and write but learning the grammar of every subject. There are basic facts belonging to every subject from history to anatomy to geography to language. Dates, capitals, presidents, battles, parts of speech, bits of poetry—these are the grammatical building blocks of an education. They all must become readily available to the mind of a young student. And these can only be acquired by extensive memorization.

To reinforce her point, Sayers also says that Grammar School comes in the one season of life when memorization is easy and often even gratifying.

> The Poll-parrot stage is the one in which learning by heart is easy and, on the whole, pleasurable; whereas reasoning is difficult and, one the whole, little relished. At his age one readily memorizes the shapes and appearances of things; one like to recite the number-plates of cars; one rejoices in the chanting of rhymes and the rumble and thunder of unintelligible polysyllables; one enjoys the mere accumulation of things.[5]

You will be amazed to hear fourth graders recite the Declaration of Independence or a whole chapter of the Sermon on the Mount. Most parents listen and think, "There is no way I could do that." That's partly because we're no longer so sponge-like and partly because memorizing is a skill. It is a huge blessing later in life when your mind has been trained to retain knowledge efficiently and effectively. The Grammar School is an incredible opportunity to capitalize on seven years of being an information sponge. Don't waste these years. Memorization is not only relevant in the Grammar School years but throughout a classical education and beyond. The muscles trained in these first years begin to prepare them for the rest of life.

There is a common parental objection to this line of reasoning: "Picturing my children sitting all day parroting a bunch of memorized facts sounds awful. How could they ever love learning with such tedium?" Though I'm not convinced that kids find this work tedious—quite the opposite—let's meet this objection halfway: Let's not have students sit. Get them up on their feet; get them moving and doing hand motions while they memorize and recite. In fact, don't have them say facts; have them sing. (After all, when they do this on the playground, it's not called work. It's called fun.)

Can you picture this incredible vision? Imagine children *singing* their whole elementary education! They'd be like the elves of Rivendell in *The Lord of the Rings*, singing with passion and wonder the stories and battles and histories of their people. These elves knew they were characters in a great epic, and they were called to play their part. Classroom songs and chants may not pierce the soul like the songs of Arwen, but a classical school should aspire to such a depth and beauty of knowledge nonetheless.

Always in the background of such a school, at any hour of the day, you'll hear children singing. Singing praise to God. Singing the presidents of the United States or the countries of western Africa. Singing the different kinds of animals that live in water. Is there any better sound to fill our halls?

The elves of Middle Earth give us another insight about memorization: *memorizing* is closely tied to *remembering*. Elven songs gave their people a collective recollection of their history. They reminded them of the great lessons of the past and instilled in them wisdom. The goal of memorization is to give a child a memory. When children memorize the basic knowledge acquired by human culture, they are inheriting the collective memory of humanity. They are learning to love their neighbor.

It's amazing to think that a seventh grader learning pre-algebra is benefitting from what the most brilliant geniuses of vast civilizations took centuries to develop. They receive in one school year perhaps a thousand years of collective wisdom. Grammar gifts a child with a powerful and well-informed memory.

Psychologists know that memory is deeply important for shaping how we live successfully in the world. Consider people who experience traumatic abuse in childhood, so that their mind blocks out most or all of their early life. They might say, "I can't remember anything before age twelve." This blackout may cut off connection with the trauma, but it also may disconnect a person from lessons learned in childhood about social cues or how to interact successfully with other people. Our memories equip us to love well and to live wisely in the world.

A society can suffer the same kind of dysfunction when cultural memory is not passed on to the children. It's like the lessons of the past are blacked out, and children are forced to navigate the world without these memories.

Memory is not simply an individual reality but also a communal one. People groups have a corporate memory. This is true of the church throughout history—the body of Christ. The Bible envisions the body of Christ (the church) as a child that is growing up, becoming more and more mature and more and more perfected in her knowledge of God's truth as the centuries pass. God gave the church teachers to build up the church

> until we all attain to the unity of the faith and of the knowledge of the Son of God, to mature manhood, to the measure of the stature of the fullness of Christ, so that we may no longer be children, tossed to and fro by the waves and carried about by every wind of doctrine. (Eph 4:13–14)

Paul says this not about individuals but about the people of God as a whole. There is a body of knowledge that the body of Christ has acquired over history, and this knowledge must be built upon in each successive generation. This only happens if the children of God's people are taught to memorize it. The loss of cultural memory is analogous to the loss of childhood memory.

This is one reason why a Christian who believes the gospel (the good news of the kingdom of Jesus coming to earth) might champion classical learning. Classical learning coheres with the Bible's understanding of God's redemptive developments in history. We are living in a great story, and our children must know what has happened in the earlier chapters of the story to understand the chapter they currently find themselves living in. Classical education does not idealize (or idolize) the past but recognizes that our hope for the future must involve building upon what we have learned in the past.

It is essential, then, both to education and to Christian discipleship, for children to memorize what God has revealed to his people in history. The ancients considered memorization more important than writing, because writing can simply be knowledge buried somewhere in a book.[6] When knowledge is memorized, however, it is always ready at hand. The disciple of Jesus must "always [be] prepared to make a defense ... for the hope that is in you" (1 Pet 3:15). That's our goal: a basic yet cohesive knowledge of God and his world living inside our children by the time they finish Grammar School.

This discussion of collective memory previews another fundamental quality of classical learning that we'll discuss in more detail later: the importance of primary sources. From the earliest ages, classical students don't just read books about the Bible. They read God's Word itself. They don't just read about the American Revolution but memorize the Declaration of Independence.

Alongside reading primary sources and memorizing the inherited cultural knowledge of the Western world is a third essential skill taught in the Grammar School.

WRITING

One of the great misconceptions of our age is that creativity largely comes from spontaneity. We have so idolized the notion of the innocent, childlike inner self that we believe brilliant creativity will just spill out of children if we will simply get out of the way and let their imaginations run free.

This is not totally wrong. Take away their screens and video games, force them to be bored for an hour, and you will often be amazed (after a bit of complaining) at the creative ways they invent entertainment for themselves.

But to truly create things that are beautiful and good requires skill. True goodness doesn't arise from our innocent inner selves but from grace and discipleship and virtue. Likewise, true skill doesn't arise haphazardly or effortlessly. We must be trained to be skillful.

My daughter once played Miss Hannigan in a children's performance of *Annie*. In the middle of the play, the stage crew was having technical difficulties, so the director told all the children to "Do something funny" to entertain the crowd while we waited for the play to resume. The crew must have shared the common assumption that children are natural wellsprings of creativity. The exercise backfired: the children all froze. As effortless as professionals make improvisation seem, it is a skill that needs to be learned with practice. Spontaneity alone cannot generate anything worth sharing.

Grammar is an art or a skill and, mainly, the skill of using words.[7] Young people can learn this art and become great with words, but we must give them the fundamental techniques if they are going to do it well. The ancients said, "Imitation precedes art." The apprentice woodworker watches his master and through repeated action becomes more and more like him. He learns rules of thumb about choosing materials and tools and how and when to use them. He must practice these actions over and over for himself until they become instinctual.

When I was first learning to preach, I would listen to seasoned pastors and try to emulate them—their word choice, their cadence, the inflection in their voices, the structure of their sermons. I'd notice the ways they were able to grab my attention and attempt those techniques myself. I gradually developed my own voice and am no longer reliant on imitation. But when I was learning, these models were invaluable.

The same is true with writing. Just as the Grammar student must read, read, read, and memorize, memorize, memorize, so they must write, write, write. Every day and every week, they will write something. In Grammar School, they're given the skills of using adjectives, relative clauses, and adverbs. Over thirteen years of primary and secondary schooling, they will write pages of essays, book reviews, creative pieces, and persuasive papers. Through this repeated action, the great skill of writing becomes more and more effortless.

These writing skills in the grammar stage are laying the foundation for the future rhetoric stage, where students practice being not just accurate but persuasive and poetic. Indeed, we might say that memory looks forward to the logic stage (discussion and dialectic) while writing looks forward to the rhetoric stage (learning to express oneself well).

Even as adults, we must not lose our wonder at the seemingly magical powers of reading, memorizing, and writing. An education in love is an education in words. Once these magic powers become effortless in our children, they are ready to try their hands at using them with precision.

Therefore, it is necessary to arrive at a first mover, put in motion by no other; and this everyone understands to be God.

Thomas Aquinas, *Summa Theologica*

7

LOGIC

Usually around twelve or thirteen, a change happens in a child. He not only starts to get pimples, but spiritually, emotionally, and mentally, he is changing as well. Cultures throughout history have known that our educational activity should be suited to our newly changing children. As they move from the Grammar School to the Logic School, they are transforming from parrots and chanters into young philosophers. It's not as if they ever fully leave grammar behind or that they have never encountered logic before. But the Logic School represents a real change nonetheless—not only in the students' readiness but also in their teachers' emphases and approach.

One of the greatest pleasures in my life is sitting at a pub with a thoughtful friend or acquaintance (whether he thinks like me or not) and talking about the deep issues of existence: ethics, relationships, culture, and above all, who is God and how do all these things relate to him? It is shocking to me how many people go through life rarely experiencing this pleasure. One thing I desire for my children is that their lives will be filled with such deep and rich conversation. I want them to know the pleasure of philosophizing.

But what makes for a good conversation? There are some important rules of thumb. You need to foster mutual respect and look for points of contact. You have to be able to listen as someone curious enough to believe someone else might say something you've never thought of (or never thought of in quite the same way). Listening means asking good questions, and there is an art to asking good questions. You have to be knowledgeable about the world but able to get to the point. A conversation needs to involve challenge and conflict but not so much that either side withdraws from the discussion. And a healthy dose of laughter always reveals that the goal of a great conversation is love.

Such conversations are the heart of the Logic School. Therefore, the culture of the Logic School is different from that of the Grammar. The structure is loosened, but the demand to think deeper is heightened. (So it shouldn't be surprising that this is also the most complex chapter in the book.) Let's focus on three areas of deep thinking at the heart of the Logic School: the centrality of history, the skills of logical reasoning, and participation in the Great Conversation.

THE CENTRALITY OF HISTORY

"Christianity," Huston Smith writes, "is basically a historical religion."[1] If we were to compare the Christian faith to the other religions of the world, we could say a lot more, but we would never want to say less. The backbone of the Bible is a historical narrative: the story of God's work in human history from creation to consummation. Read the opening lines of the Qur'an and the Bible, and they will tell you immediately the kind of book you are about to read. The Qur'an is a book of instructions for how to submit to

God. It begins, “This is the Scripture in which there is no doubt, containing guidance for those who are mindful of God.” The Bible is a story about the history of God’s work in the world. It begins, “In the beginning, God created the heavens and the earth.” Near the very start of the Bible’s story, God gives us history’s main storyline:

> The LORD God said to the serpent … “I will put enmity between you and the woman, and between your offspring and her offspring; he shall bruise your head, and you shall bruise his heel.” (Gen 3:14–15)

Immediately after the fall of humanity, almost the first word out of God’s mouth is the promise of a Savior—the Seed of the woman who would suffer in great conflict with the Serpent but ultimately crush his head. The Old and New Testaments tell the story of how in history this prophecy has been fulfilled and how it will come to perfect completion in the future. For Christians, then, history is centrally about how Jesus’s victory over evil has unfolded during and after the age of the Bible.[2]

When Christ and God’s Word are at the heart of an education, history will be central. This is also why classical education puts such an emphasis on Western civilization. In God’s providence, it turns out that the pathway of the gospel—the transformative message about Jesus—has enjoyed its most thorough development in the West. This is by no means a favoring of European or white peoples because clearly, the love of God in the gospel is indiscriminately for all nations. Augustine, the greatest mind outside the Bible in the formation of the Western world, was an African. Our Lord has always had a vision for all the people groups of the world. Indeed, the gospel made significant inroads into the Middle East, Africa, and Asia during the first thousand years of the church.[3] As things are currently trending, the next Christendom of the third millennium will likely be in Africa or

Asia or other regions of the majority world where Christianity is expanding at exponential rates.[4]

But for the first two thousand years of the coming of Christ's kingdom to earth, its most far-reaching and uninterrupted cultural impact has been in the Western world. Though the West is riddled with all the sins of other cultures (greed, oppression, violence, injustice), the gospel has borne undeniably bountiful fruit: in learning, in justice, in government, in economics, in the arts, and in medicine.

This is so important to affirm in our day. Modern progressive secularism assumes the myth that humanity is constantly improving itself through science and technology, independent of Jesus Christ or really any inherited tradition of wisdom. It sees the present as inherently more enlightened than the past. The Bible is on the wrong side of history. (Such a belief is, of course, self-defeating: If it were true, it would mean in a hundred years, when our generation is long gone, today's newest insights will inevitably become tomorrow's ignorance.) Nevertheless, in this fashion, modern secularism has attempted to frame Christianity and the church as both oppressive and regressive. But nothing could be further from the truth.

The gospel first emerged in the cities of the Roman Empire, as we read in the book of Acts. During the next centuries, Christians so shaped the culture and ethics of their world that even the emperor Constantine was finally converted in the fourth century. But Rome was even more deeply shaped by pagan brutality and sensuality. At the fall of the Roman Empire in the fifth century, it seemed as if God was laying the world bare again. The Mediterranean world and Europe were like a new wasteland, formless and void.[5] Many Christians lamented the decadence and decay of Rome; some moved into the desert and began monasteries and churches in the wild world of uncivilized Western Europe.

For the next four hundred years, they ventured into brutal barbarian lands with simply a book, water for baptizing, and bread and wine for communing. These meek yet ambitious missionaries told pagan kings about the love of Jesus, and, amazingly, many believed. The barbarian kings gifted lands to bishops and asked priests to educate their people.[6] These small outposts of spirituality, learning, and mercy in the middle of the so-called Dark Ages were the beginning of the remaking of their world.

In the eighth and ninth centuries, Charlemagne of the Franks and then Alfred the Great of England built—certainly imperfect—kingdoms upon the foundation of these monasteries and the worldview of the gospel, teaching a Christ-centered life to common people through the church.[7] At the center of both their reforms was education. "To convert was to educate," according to historian Tom Holland. "This, the great lesson taught by Boniface, was one that the Franks would not forget."[8] Such cultural innovations led to the governmental and intellectual developments of the medieval period. Basic human rights were affirmed and research universities were established. The empirical mind of modern science was forged in the scholasticism of Thomas Aquinas and the orderly thinking of the medievals.[9]

During the Reformation, as Christians again returned to a deep study of the gospel, Europe enjoyed massive innovations in government, economics and commerce, public education, and literature and the arts. No area of the culture was left untouched. In the centuries that followed, they abolished slavery, built the greatest colleges in the world, cared for the poor and the children of the poor, and sent missionaries to the four corners of the earth. None of this came from spotless motives or led to perfect outcomes, of course. My point is that history shows us the gospel really does bear fruit beyond private, individual spirituality—it's a world-making power.

In the twentieth century, Christianity expanded like never before in China, Africa, and South America. Nevertheless, it has steadily died out in Europe and other parts of the West. What should we make of this? On one hand, we can acknowledge that it's consistent with the God we meet in the Bible: When one people group rejects him, he takes his grace to others who are eager to receive his Word.

On the other hand, this reminds us to be careful when trying to understand history. God's Word is his divinely inspired interpretation of the world's story, and it paints for us the broad arc of the story God is writing in history. It also gives us many examples and principles that can make us wise interpreters of history. But much of God's providence remains mysterious. We generally can't know God's precise purposes outside of biblical revelation. For example, we can know for certain that God raised up Cyrus the Persian for the purpose of restoring Israel from exile. We cannot say with such confidence the same for Charlemagne.

The people who represent Western civilization in history all suffered from total depravity like everyone else. And it's all too easy to project our own personal biases onto historical figures, canonizing some while vilifying others. We often want to justify ourselves, but rarely can our interpretation of history be so clean-cut.

What the Christian student must come to internalize is that Jesus Christ is the one building a global civilization on the earth: the City of God. The gospel is always a fresh and surprising force that brings life and creativity and freedom to the world. History is moving toward the glorious kingdom of God in the future. Despite the great sinfulness of humanity—even of committed Christians—our Lord has been, and continues to be, working all things for the good of his people (Rom 8:28). So, the only way we can creatively and faithfully move into the future is by building on what Jesus has done among his people in the past.

Christians have certainly done many evil things, and even our best works enjoy mixed results. The Bible itself acknowledges this sad truth of a fallen world. Nevertheless, the very idea of progress comes from Christianity. The Bible casts the golden age of humanity not as a lost tradition of the past but as the kingdom of God coming over time, which will only be fully realized in the future.

How is this vision different from secular versions of progress? There are two main differences. First, the kingdom of God is not a work of man's ingenuity but a gift of God's grace. As our Lord told his disciples, "It is your Father's good pleasure to give you the kingdom" (Luke 12:32). That is why Jesus teaches his disciples to pray for this vision of human history to come, since the King is the only one who can build his kingdom on the earth. "Your kingdom come, your will be done, on earth as it is in heaven" (Matt 6:10).

Second, the gospel tells us that progress toward glory is always and only through the suffering of the cross. The story arc of human history leads through death to resurrection. Humanity is not on a steady upward trajectory of self-improvement. The inner logic of Christian progress—both personal and communal—is to die with Christ in order to find new life in him. As G. K. Chesterton put it,

> Christendom has had a series of revolutions and in each one of them Christianity has died. Christianity has died many times and risen again; for it had a God who knew the way out of the grave. ... The Faith is always converting the age, not as an old religion but as a new religion.[10]

At no point in history can Christians look on the past with arrogance. We must always engage the world around us with humility and hope.

It is so important that we don't miss the story in history. Human history is made up of the stories of countless people living various lives in a mixture of sin and righteousness, from which you and I get to learn vicariously. Just as wise people reflect on their own personal histories and gradually over time begin to discern the lessons and purposes that Jesus had been authoring in their stories all along, we do the same with all human history. Over time, the old saint becomes wise because he has carefully reflected on the meaning of his own story. What would he have done differently? How did God use those decisions for his own purposes? Who were the key influences on his personality? Classical history students are beginning to do the same, not just in their own personal stories but with those of many other fascinating figures besides.

This is not the vision of history that many of us grew up with. For many late-modern people like me, we assume our time is more progressive (however that is defined) and therefore better than whatever had come before. History, meanwhile, seemed a random collection of events floating around in a foggy past. It didn't fit together into a coherent story, and so it was hard to appreciate why it mattered or what it meant.

When we understand that Jesus is the one bringing his kingdom, not us, this frees us to engage critically with fellow Christians both in the past and in the present. Christian parents and educators must regularly name sin for what it is—both those of the past and our own. Our forebears have had many blindspots, yet Jesus has worked through their weaknesses. We have many blindspots now too (often different from those in the past), so we need to look to the past to realize the things we can't see about ourselves.

Ultimately, history is vital to Christian formation in love because history is about the Son of God bringing his love to a broken, dark, and sinful world. We're living in a love story! In the Grammar School, students memorize historical dates and names and anecdotes. In the Logic School, they begin to discuss how all these events fit together in the epic tale of the kingdom. How does a student learn to put these pieces together properly?

THE SKILLS OF LOGICAL REASONING

This is precisely what the Logic School fosters: weighing information, making appropriate connections, and putting the pieces together in pursuit of wisdom. The Logic School turns each classroom into an incubator for reasoning, discussion, and debate, like a miniature parliament or even a small society. These young philosophers must begin to form opinions and attempt to defend them. Whenever a class settles on a simplistic answer to a difficult question, the teacher is there to unsettle students' assumptions and lead them to wrestle with the ordered complexity of God's world.

This ordered complexity is why the skills of logic are a key ingredient in classical learning. Because real life is complex yet ordered, so the character of classical education must be. If the rules of logic stay siloed in a formal logic class, it will largely be a wasted opportunity for the rest of the curriculum. What matters more is the thousand ways these rules are employed during every classroom conversation. Students need the vocabulary of *ad hominem* fallacies and *non sequiturs* (among many others) in order to reason well and guard against errors in their thinking in every subject. Each time in debate a student is asked to clearly state their postulates or to infer a contrapositive, for example, the tools of logic become more and more instinctual through repeated use.

Now, parents of classical students, I must warn you: you might be caught off guard when your children want to exercise their new powers of logic on *you*. These can be sanctifying conversations for both parties! Parents have to learn the humility to listen to their children's often immature ideas (and even learn from them). Students, likewise, must have the humility to recognize that, even if their parents can't perfectly articulate their reasoning, it's wise for young people to obey their parents and respect their elders in the Lord. Logic must always serve love.

As students begin to engage the complexity of God's world, they will begin to see the repeated pattern that God and his way—that is, theology—is always *paradoxical*. God is one being in three persons. Jesus is fully God and fully man. God controls every detail of every moment of his creation ("Not one [sparrow] will fall to the ground apart from your Father" [Matt 10:29]), and yet, humans are not robots but responsible for our actions and free to act according to our desires. I could go on, but the point is: All fundamental theological beliefs in the Bible are paradoxical.[11]

Paradox does not mean *contradiction*. God isn't one in the same way that he's three, just like an apple cannot be green and not green in the very same sense at the same time. Nor is a paradox a *compromise*. God isn't half-loving and half-righteous. He's fully loving and fully righteous at the same time.

Such paradoxes don't just appear in theology but in all of life. Christians must stand against abortion while also wanting to expand opportunities for women to use their God-given gifts in the world and be paid fairly for their work. The government must order society well while letting people live free lives.

The study of these paradoxes in the Logic School is called *dialectic*. The Logic School teacher will regularly divide the class into the two sides of the paradox—creating an apparent conflict—and a great conversation emerges. These conversations help students to learn the essential skill of carefully navigating the world's paradoxical truths.

Let them take sides. Force them to listen to those opposing them. Don't let them get frustrated and give up: "Well, I guess there is no answer!"

Because of our human desire for mastery and godlike control, we don't naturally like to accept paradox. Paradoxes call us to embrace the fact that two seemingly opposite things are both the truth and so we should fully affirm them both. Paradox forces us to humbly admit, "I know these things are true, but I don't fully understand how." The key word here is *humbly*.

"Why?" is probably the most philosophical question in life. When a seventh grader asks, "Why can't I stay up late?" he's really saying in his own simple way, "You've imposed a law that significantly impedes my freedom. I'd like to understand the moral rationale that justifies such an action." Every "why" invites a conversation. I've mentioned that the arrival of adolescence is often accompanied by a desire to start arguing—but rarely is that desire accompanied by humility. It's often difficult to engage a teenager's "whys" because they're so frequently self-justifying and inconsiderate. Or we don't have the time, energy, or patience to journey down those winding paths, so we shut down the conversation: "Because I said so." But grace moves us toward our children in this otherwise intolerable phase—and indeed, hidden in those "whys" is a real opportunity.

When a young person has read the great minds of the Western canon and wrestled with the mysteries of God in paradox, the trend should be toward growth in humility and depth in worship. If classical learning is a training in wisdom, then the truly wise student will wrestle with the ordered complexity of the world and the dialectical process of discovering truth in such a way as to be led to trust and praise the God who is alone all-wise. She will lean not on her own understanding but on Jesus Christ in whom all paradoxes hold together (Col 1:17).

Nevertheless, as they converse, Logic students will inevitably say all kinds of foolish things. They don't yet know how to discuss and debate well. Learning how is the third element of the Logic School.

THE GREAT CONVERSATION

I mentioned in the last chapter that the liberal arts curriculum is largely built around primary sources. There are many benefits to this. The main benefit is that, by reading primary sources, students enter into the Great Conversation that human beings have been having for thousands of years about who we are and how we should live. In this way, classical education is structured around the deepest and most lasting questions of life: What is morality? What is freedom? How much power should a government have? Why is a human life valuable? As the apostle Paul said,

> Whatever is true, whatever is honorable, whatever is just, whatever is pure, whatever is lovely, whatever is commendable, if there is any excellence, if there is anything worthy of praise, think about these things. (Phil 4:8)

Many of the greatest Christian minds from Augustine to Calvin have recommended reading not just Christian authors but pagan and unbelieving ones as well.[12] All truth is God's truth. God shows his common grace to all people (Matt 5:45), which means all kinds of writers have been given blessings to share with us—from Aristotle to Confucius. Just as the Israelites left Egypt carrying Egyptian treasure, we should plunder the riches of the unbelieving past from Plato to Nietzsche.

In our school, this Great Conversation happens in the humanities block. The humanities block wraps into one course literature, history, writing, speech, geography, logic, and theology. Each year is structured around a period of history (Ancient, Medieval,

Modern), and each unit is structured around a piece of literature (mostly primary sources). If a class spends two weeks studying *Othello*, the core content will be an interaction with the text itself. But this will lead into discussions on the biblical view of marriage (the godly Desdemona marries Othello without her father's blessing) and racism (both the racial slurs in the play as well as Shakespeare's turning of racial assumptions on their head). Students will learn about the political turmoil of England in Shakespeare's day. They'll draw maps based on the geography in which the play takes place, including the Ottoman Empire, Cyprus, Venice, and Maghreb (the geography of the play). They'll even try their hand at composing a Shakespearean sonnet. Just stop to ponder all the important subjects touched upon by a single piece of old literature!

The Great Conversation is also a guard against Christian schools becoming sanitized fortresses from the sins of the world. Reading the Western canon will require middle schoolers to come to terms with such grave topics as slavery, rape, racism, and violence. In *Othello*, they'll encounter the euphemism of a man and woman who "make the beast with two backs"; in Herodotus, they will witness the brutality of a civilization not yet touched by the love of Christ. This exposure must be handled responsibly, but it can't be avoided because real life can't be avoided. Logic students can't be completely protected from the depravity of humanity because that same depravity lives in their own hearts.

The liberal arts assume that being a philosopher is a nonnegotiable. Whether as a worshiper, a parent, a friend, a worker, or a citizen, each vocation requires us to be philosophers skilled in reasoning well. This skill is especially valuable in a culture that has come not only to think that the Bible is unhistorical and unscientific but immoral. You cannot be a thoughtful Christian in our post-Christian culture without being a philosopher. Many Christians who have not intellectually fortified themselves against the spirit of this age will struggle to keep their faith.

Logic students' "why" questions will eventually lead them to their deepest assumptions about the world. True learning only happens when our assumptions are disrupted. But this isn't always good; unsettling someone's assumptions is a dangerous business. Many young people who've grown up in the church abandon their faith because it's founded on false premises. All authority is ultimately based on God's Word since there cannot be any more trustworthy authority than God himself. Chesterton put it this way:

> Every argument begins with an infallible dogma, and that infallible dogma can only be disputed by falling back on some other infallible dogma; you can never prove your first statement or it would not be your first. All this is the alphabet of thinking. And it has this special and positive point about it, that it can be taught in a school, like the other alphabet.[13]

Not trusting the Bible as the deepest and most reliable source of truth means trusting something else as the most reliable source of truth.[14] We might trust contemporary scientists or historians or our own intuition—all of which have frequently proven unreliable—but "Why?" will always lead us to our deepest assumptions about the world.

The beautiful opportunity of the gospel-centered, classical school is that students will find again and again that every string of "whys" ends with our Lord Jesus. Christians have a deep and beautiful why for everything. He is the why behind history, morality, the arts, and all of human life. There is no more reliable "why" to build our knowledge upon. Healthy growth only happens by asking our "whys" alongside and within a support structure that leads from disrupted assumptions to deeper understanding in Christ. Why, for example, do we believe the Bible is the inerrant Word of God? Because Jesus believed so, and I trust no one more than him.

One of the supreme blessings of being a parent of classical Christian school students is experiencing the ways the Great Conversation happening in the classroom spills over onto the dining room table. My pleasure in deep conversation is now something I get to enjoy with my own children. They're sharpening my thinking and helping me to understand why I believe what I do. Learning from your own child is one of the most supremely satisfying experiences in life.

In the Logic School, our students are making connections, engaging history in meaningful conversation, learning to live in paradox, and speaking in their own words the deep mysteries of the world. Their minds are beginning to be strengthened and sharpened by logic.

Still, we've all met that guy who can masterfully prove how right he is—while no one can stand talking to him. We should never wish such an educational outcome upon anyone, especially classical Christian school students! This is why the capstone of the Trivium must go beyond grammar and logic to rhetoric: the wise and loving skill of persuasive communication.

The wisdom of what a person says is in direct proportion to his progress in learning the Holy Scriptures—and I am not speaking of intensive reading or memorization, but real understanding and careful investigation of their meaning.

St. Augustine, *On Christian Teaching*

8

RHETORIC

There is no power like that of words. Swords or guns can make men act against their wills, but words have a power that physical force never will. Words reach inside of us and shape who we are. They have power not to *force* the will but power to *form* the will. Nothing inspires, motivates, and challenges a human being like the right words, spoken in the right way, at the right time. Words can crush with shame or reverse the course of a lost life.

The ability to communicate well is the most powerful adult human skill and yet—increasingly—young people aren't being trained in it. Classical schools understand this and want our students to be the ones who go out into the world and shape the culture more than they're shaped by it. Since cultures are created largely through words, the capstone of the classical school is rhetoric: the ability to move others with our words. This isn't a natural ability but a skill to be learned. In any vocation—teacher, entrepreneur, mother, firefighter, nurse, lawyer, citizen, Christian—using words well is perhaps *the key skill* for effectiveness and influence.

If Christian students are to be Christ's witnesses carrying his grace and wisdom into every part of their lives, they must learn to communicate with clarity, humility, and conviction. They must be confident and warm, winsome and compelling, their thoughts presented with both order and beauty.

After the spiritual formation of a student, therefore, rhetoric is the second highest goal of a gospel-centered classical education. Because rhetoric is one of the highest goals in classical learning, the final stage of secondary education (high school) is often referred to as the Rhetoric School. Just as the Grammar School involves some logic training and the Logic School never really leaves grammar behind, so rhetoric to some degree has been present in a classical school student's training all along. Even kindergarteners, for example, must regularly stand before their peers—Head up! Shoulders back! Project your voice!—to practice public speaking. Rhetoric builds on the skills learned in grammar and logic, bringing them to useful fruition. It equips students not only to join but to contribute to the Great Conversation. The Grammar and Logic Schools have been their athletic exercises and drills; Rhetoric School is game time. (To cut off classical education after eighth grade, then, is like asking players to enter the competitive arena of life without ever playing any practice games.) Classical education keeps the end in view from the very beginning.

Like almost everything in the Christian life, when you put the glory of God first, often a blessed life gets thrown in as a bonus. Serve your neighbors with excellence through your business because that's honoring to God, and often the business will grow. Put your spouse's needs above your own in obedience to God, and you'll often find yourself with a happier marriage. Rhetoric training works the same way. If there's one activity that human beings perform all the time—and so have great reason to be good at—it's communicating. Teach young people to speak and write well so they can understand and articulate their convictions effectively, and it turns out you are giving them the strongest tool for success in almost any future vocation. "The lips of the righteous feed many" (Prov 10:21).

But more important than being a world-changer (as grand as that sounds) is that using words well is essential for loving well. One of the primary ways we will love others is with our words. God loves us with his Word; husbands love their wives with their words (Eph 5:26); friends love each other by talking. Words are how we comfort, encourage, teach, correct, and express our concerns and our delights. Training in love is an education in rhetoric because love always strives to bring grace and truth into the deepest recesses of the human heart.

So what contributes to such effective expression? What are the key elements of rhetoric?

PERSUASION: USING BEAUTIFUL WORDS POWERFULLY

The whole idea of rhetoric is often met with suspicion in the modern world. We hear a politician's speech and dismiss it as "just a bunch of rhetoric." We think of rhetoric as empty words masking a lack of real results or a form of verbal manipulation—saying things in a sophisticated or clever way just to get people to think or do what we want.

The Bible shares this suspicion to some degree. The apostle Paul uses this contrast when describing his own public teaching ministry:

> I ... did not come proclaiming to you the testimony of God with lofty speech or wisdom. ...I was with you in weakness and in fear and much trembling, and my speech and my message were not in plausible words of wisdom, but in demonstration of the Spirit and of power. (1 Cor 2:1, 3–4)

Paul is just as repelled by empty talk and emotional exploitation as we are.

At the same time, any student of Paul's letters knows he constantly employs powerful rhetorical skills. He had been trained at a Roman school in Damascus; he uses his words skillfully to build arguments and bring them home to the hearts of his readers. In fact, in his second letter to the Corinthians, he says, "Knowing the fear of the Lord, we persuade others" (2 Cor 5:11). He summarizes his whole calling, in some sense, as a mission of persuasion.

So what's the difference between Paul the persuasive preacher and the manipulative rhetoricians he criticizes? The difference is character: He persuades while "knowing the fear of the Lord." So when Paul says he spoke with "weakness" and "fear," he's basically saying, "I came to you with the humility of Christ. My life and manner match my message." Paul is suspicious of worldly rhetoric precisely because he knows rhetoric is such a powerful skill—both in the right hands and in the wrong hands.

Isn't this why the first goal of a classical Christian school should be training our students in Christ's love so that his character will be formed in them? Rhetoric is a kind of manipulation, it's true. But as C. S. Lewis has pointed out, it's not wrong to want to be "manipulated" by godly teachers.[1] We want them to convince us to trust God and do what's right, don't we? We want them to move us, steering our emotions toward what's beautiful, good, and true. It's an immense blessing to be persuaded by someone who's good and wise.

In fact, Aristotle said a speaker's character is the *most* persuasive part of his or her communication:

> It is not true, as some writers assume in their treatises on rhetoric, that the personal goodness revealed by the speaker contributes nothing to his power of persuasion; on

> the contrary, his character may almost be called the most effective means of persuasion he possesses.[2]

Aristotle called this persuasive character of a communicator his *ethos*. Alongside *ethos*, Aristotle identifies two other means of persuasion any successful speaker must employ: *pathos* (speaking to the emotions) and *logos* (reasoning effectively).

We develop *pathos* through practice in listening to and speaking with others. Do you know how the Beatles learned to stir the emotions of an entire generation through their music? They spent three years touring before their first album, playing shows in front of young people—primarily in Hamburg, Germany—almost every night. By 1964, they had played twelve hundred shows. They learned what melodies and choruses made the fans scream.[3] You only learn to speak to the emotions by speaking in front of actual people to see what moves them.

Similarly, we develop *logos* through practice in reasoning with others. A compelling presentation or speech, for example, should have a clear thesis, with everything else related to that thesis. Imagine if someone listening in the audience were to raise her hand to disagree—what might she say? A skillful reasoner will anticipate such objections, articulate them, and answer them with truth and grace.

The combination of these three qualities of *ethos*, *pathos*, and *logos* is incredibly powerful, and the classical Christian school helps to shape all three. As students give speeches, write thesis papers, and conduct debates, they are constantly evaluated against these three qualities. Can you imagine a greater lifelong gift to give to young people? I want my children to be able to speak effectively to others' hearts. This isn't only important if they become preachers or politicians. It's essential to being a parent or a business owner or a nurse. It's essential to being a mature Christian who disciples others. What a blessing to the world and culture around us—young people with the character of Christ, speaking persuasively to the hearts and minds of their neighbors about what is true and good and beautiful!

Communicating this way does not come effortlessly. Whether a comedian or a CEO, anyone who speaks publicly will tell you that developing rhetorical power demands patient labor. How do students learn to synthesize so many data points, ideas, and arguments into persuasive speeches or essays that not only relay information but move their hearers and leave them changed? Such creative work is impossible without careful reflection.

CONTEMPLATION: REFLECTING ON THE TRUTH

Deep into Augustine's magnum opus, *The City of God*, he makes an observation about the value of both action and reflection:

> No man has a right to lead such a life of contemplation as to forget in his own ease the service due to his neighbor; nor has any man a right to be so immersed in active life as to neglect the contemplation of God.[4]

The wise and the persuasive have learned not just to be active in doing good but to reflect on what is good, beautiful, and true. John Calvin also said that there are two great objects of contemplation for the human being: God and ourselves. We can't know one without the other. This also means that only by contemplating Jesus—fully God and fully man—do we truly understand the subtle complexities of our tragic sinfulness and of God's amazing grace.

The famous Roman orator Quintilian developed laboratories for training his students in rhetoric. Contemplation was vital to his method:

> No man will ever be thoroughly accomplished in eloquence who has not gained a deep insight into the impulses of human nature and formed his moral character on the precepts of others and on his own reflection.[5]

The ability to persuade others flows from a place of deep personal reflection and conviction. It comes from contemplation of the mysteries of God and his world and of human motivations (whether others' or our own). In this quiet, patient discipline, thinking becomes clear, insights emerge, and knowledge distills into wisdom.[6]

The classical Christian school shouldn't feel like a factory efficiently stamping out identical products but a garden carefully cultivating a variety of species. The unique flower that is each student emerges only through contemplation. The gardeners (the teachers) should know each plant and what kind of climate and care best suits its fruitfulness.

The modern worldview has treated the universe more like a machine, so it's no wonder government schools have tended to operate in the same way. Machines can be sophisticated, impressive, and expensive. But even when well-oiled and in good working order, they're still rigid and artificial—and relentless. C. S. Lewis described the sorry state of the typical student:

> He has hardly ever been alone. The educational machine seizes him very early and organizes his whole life, to the exclusion of all unsuperintended solitude or leisure. The hours of unsponsored, uninspected, perhaps even forbidden, reading, the ramblings, and the "long, long thoughts" in which those of luckier generations first discovered literature and nature and themselves are a thing of the past.[7]

Contemplative solitude is increasingly valuable and increasingly rare in the frenzy of late modern life.

The real world isn't like a machine. It's more like a story or a living thing. Reality is filled with countless wonders: blue whales, black holes, winding rivers, subatomic particles, talking animals. (In case you're wondering, you are the talking animal.) To learn about such a wild and surprising world, students' minds must have space for wonder and imagination to hold sway.

If parents and schools are going to encourage contemplation, we must constantly guard against two dangers. First, the demands of the modern private school, with all of the expectations of perfectionism and achievement, have filled the child's hours with "productivity." Childhood is losing the wastefulness that historically was essential for true enjoyment. Wastefulness is a part of what is good and true and beautiful about God. The Lord enjoys many things in his creation that often seem, to us, inefficient—whether it's the thousands of cherries that fall to the ground or are eaten that will never become a new tree, or the trillions of stars and planets that humans will never know existed. The Lord's purposes in redemption even take millennia to unfold. He seems so unhurried. Efficiency is a low priority. A thousand years are like a day when it is past (Ps 90:4).

If our children are to become like their Maker, they need some un-hurry. It is in the unhurriedness of contemplation that true wisdom can emerge.

The second danger, though, is that our children's "unsuperintended solitude" is constantly being invaded by cheap, shallow distractions like binge-watching shows or endless gaming. TV and video games aren't sinful, but they don't foster the "long, long thoughts" of contemplation that Lewis encourages. Just as an adult who wishes to accomplish deep work must carve out long periods of time uninterrupted by email or news or social media, so young people must have protected time devoted to contemplation. In our school, the children are in class Monday to Thursday, while Friday is a homeschool day reserved for deep work and contemplation. Especially as students move into the Rhetoric School, this home day is more and more focused on creative writing and poring over great works of literature. There's simply no substitute for slowly working through and synthesizing their thoughts into a persuasive paper or speech.

Students thrive with space to explore a challenging math problem or write a new piece of code. In these hours of contemplation, another rhetorical ability begins to form in these young hearts and minds. It's a tacit knowledge, a sensitivity, an intuitive work of the imagination some have called *poetic knowledge.*[8]

POETICS: GAINING A TASTE FOR GOODNESS

If you're a particularly intuitive person, you often can't describe how you know certain things. Where did that insight come from? "I just felt it in my gut." How did you discern that error? "I sensed deeply that something wasn't right." This intuition about goodness, beauty, and truth is poetic knowledge. The ability to synthesize many sources of information, to tease out valuable insights, or even to connect with someone emotionally often comes down to intuition more than analysis.

If we're wise, of course, we've learned long ago to be suspicious of our intuitions. Intuition is powerful but imprecise and often wrong. Some intuitions are knee-jerk reactions that lead us away from true insight and discernment. Intuition must be trained.

One of the most powerful ways of training our intuition is through reading the work of those who are skilled and wise in poetic knowledge. How can anyone help others taste the sweetness of something if he hasn't first tasted it himself? Classical literature (especially poetry) has endured for so many generations and crossed so many cultures because of its ability to capture the subtlety of the human condition and the sublimity of the created order.

Such rich works are acquired tastes, however, and most modern students have not yet made the acquisition. Flannery O'Connor is direct on this point:

> If the student finds [classic literature] not to his taste? Well, that is regrettable. Most regrettable. His taste should not be consulted; it is being formed.[9]

Poetic taste is like culinary taste. My wife and I have told our children they're allowed to refuse to eat one food—and that's it. To let them turn their nose up at the wide world of edibles—mushrooms, lambs, chimichurri sauces, poached eggs—is to cut them off from a whole realm of pleasures. I want their lives to be as filled with healthy pleasures as possible. It's all the more proof that God is generous and more reason for them to give him thanks.

Likewise, a Rhetoric School student must be persuaded (manipulated?) to dive into George Herbert like a toddler is made to eat roasted broccoli. The more they taste delicious literature, the more they'll learn intuitively to judge what's good and what's not—what works and what doesn't.

Philosophers have said historically that proportion is one of the most essential ingredients for beauty. We experience a face or a composition as beautiful when it is well proportioned. Cooking delicious food involves combining the right proportions of acid, fat, salt, spice, and texture. The more good food you've eaten, the better you'll know when something is too much or is missing.

The Bible uses a similar idea to talk about the wisdom of God and how he acts in the world. The word is "fitting." Proverbs says of the wise: "A word fitly spoken is like apples of gold in a setting of silver" (25:11). Fittingness is about setting. It is about knowing what fits, in what context, and with just the right amount of truth and grace, logic and emotion, simplicity and complexity, humor and gravity. Rhetorical skill requires experience with poetics in order to gain these same sensibilities for effective communication.

The story of the Bible—and so the story of the whole world—is a masterpiece of fittingness. At its center is the most poetic turn of proportion and fittingness, a dramatic climax that fills us with fear, wonder, gratitude, and pleasure. The book of Hebrews captures it brilliantly:

> For it was fitting that he, for whom and by whom all things exist, in bringing many sons to glory, should make the founder of their salvation perfect through suffering. (Heb 2:10)

In the cross, love and death—the ultimate realities of human existence—collide into a single moment of matchless devotion and senseless injustice. And through this surprising turn, the world is saved.

Jesus is the full embodiment of goodness, beauty, and truth. He is perfect persuasion; his *ethos*, *pathos*, and *logos* have captured billions of hearts throughout history and continue to do so today. The drama of the cross is the majestic collision of mercy and justice, grace and truth, love and judgment. It is the key that perfectly fits all the locked doors of human life and nature itself. There's something so attractive about Jesus that even many who aren't Christians and don't like religion are still fascinated by him.

The gospel is also strange and mysterious. Even though Jesus is the fullness of goodness, beauty, and truth, we're told that his meekness, lowliness, and poverty made him seem ugly to us (Isa 53:2–3). Humanly speaking, his death was not an act of goodness but the greatest single act of injustice ever committed. The trial that led to his death wasn't full of truth but brimming with falsehoods. Yet through Jesus's ugliness, injustices, and slanders, he becomes the setting that makes our lives beautiful. His imperfection becomes our true perfection. "For our sake he made him to be sin who knew no sin, so that in him we might become the righteousness of God" (2 Cor 5:21). For those with "ears to hear," as Jesus often puts it, there's no rhetoric more surprising yet compelling than rhetoric shaped from beginning to end by the message of the gospel.

This surprising yet compelling quality of gospel rhetoric can only flow from students who are likewise shaped by this gospel. Rhetoric exists for serving others in love. This is why it's usually not the polished speaker who moves us but the sincere person speaking an honest word from the heart. High rhetoric or cultural elitism aren't prerequisites for being a faithful follower of Jesus. Jesus turns on its head the pretension of rhetorical subtlety. "If I speak in the tongues of men and of angels," Paul says, "but have not love, I am a noisy gong or a clanging cymbal" (1 Cor 13:1). We must find God's beauty in "the poor in spirit"—as classical Christian school students should be—for Jesus has given his kingdom to people like these (Matt 5:3).

The deepest poetic intuition comes from the contemplation of these mysteries of gospel grace. And so again, this chapter leads us back to our thesis: Gospel education is a training in the love of Jesus. The Rhetoric School forms students in his subtle and poetic love—in the fittingness of his words and deeds. The more our students taste the sweetness of that love, the more they will become men and women whose *ethos* is Christlike, whose *pathos* is genuine and humble, and whose *logos* is as clear, careful, and honest as glass—that they may be clear windows through whom the light of Christ can shine.

In your true belief about the world's government—that it is subject to divine reason and not the haphazards of chance—there lies our greatest hope of rekindling your health.

Boethius, *The Consolation of Philosophy*

9

MATH & SCIENCE

For many people, the last word that comes to mind in connection with love is *math*. I suspect this is because the same thing that keeps us from love in every other area of life has blocked our love in mathematics too: fear. We shouldn't blame anyone for trembling when they venture into the holy realm of the beautifully mathematical mind of God. We should expect seventh-grade boys and girls (and maybe their parents) to feel their smallness before the rational order of the cosmos. Who wouldn't be humbled by approaching such mysteries? But if the greatest obstacle in math is legitimate fear, what's the solution?

Before being called to ministry, I was studying to be a mathematician. Once, in an orientation at the start of my doctoral program, the facilitator began, "You cannot get a PhD in math unless ... "—what words did I expect next? Unless you're unusually brilliant? Unless you're coldly logical? No—"*Unless you love it*." Only love unlocks new worlds of infinite dimensional vector spaces, leading us into undiscovered numerical realms. It didn't take long to realize he was right, and in hindsight, his words shouldn't have been surprising to me. The Bible tells us that "perfect love casts out fear" (1 John 4:18). As it turns out, this is no less true in trigonometry than in salvation.

FOR THE LOVE OF MATH

The greatest teacher I ever had wasn't a Christian. I'm pretty sure he was an atheist. But was he ever captured by the beauty of math! I'd never encountered someone who experienced a proof like a story, full of drama and suspense. Mathematical objects were like characters with personalities—some heroes, some foes. He was meticulous about the chalk he used (only a variety of colors would do), and he often smashed the chalk against the board for dramatic effect.

My professor was also particular about clear handwriting and the aesthetic quality of mathematical symbols. He thought proofs should be elegant and orderly. Real numbers were x, y, and z; natural numbers n, m, and k; linear transforms were uppercase letters like T and S. "God is not a God of confusion. ... All things should be done decently and in order" (1 Cor 14:33, 40). One of my fellow graduate students would often present to our class proofs on the chalkboard that were a total mess. We learned to realize even before analyzing them, "There must be errors buried in here somewhere." My professor trained me to see disorder as a way of masking ignorance. (My children will tell you that, even now, few things get me going more than a disorderly math problem.) Order, in contrast, is a way of being transparent. It's like the difference between an intact pane of glass and a fractured one. When the crystalline structure in the glass is aligned, light can pass freely through it. When it's broken, so is our ability to see.

As mentioned earlier, the liberal arts are divided into two parts: the Trivium and the Quadrivium. The Trivium consists of the arts of language (grammar, logic, and rhetoric). We now move to the Quadrivium (arithmetic, geometry, astronomy, and music), which mainly consists of math. Arithmetic and geometry are traditionally mathematical subjects concerning number and shape, while music is math applied to sound and astronomy is math applied to space.

In modern classical schools, the Quadrivium not only focuses on astronomy but science more broadly (earth sciences, physics, chemistry, and biology in the secondary school). The ancients tended to study the heavens as the place of certainty and clarity (the stars moving in their "fixed courses"), but they saw the earth as a place of chaos and uncertainty and therefore tended to place a higher value on the study of the heavens.[1] In the early modern era (especially in the wake of the Calvinist revolution), we increasingly saw the whole universe as governed by the same wise and sovereign providence, equally on the earth as among the stars. So, we increasingly began to recognize the value of bringing mathematical and scientific study to bear here below.[2]

In this chapter, we'll see why a classical school shaped by Jesus will put a special emphasis on the Quadrivium and reflect on how math and science relate to the gospel. Indeed, one of the primary purposes of teaching math is to train a young mind to love the beauty and order of the Logos of the universe: the Son of God himself.

THE BEAUTY OF ORDER

Doing math well requires a certain conscientiousness akin to the carefulness of love. Just as a gentle and faithful husband is purposeful with his words and reliable in his actions, the Lord of heaven and earth is careful and predictable in how he governs the universe. Math is the conscientious and orderly way of the Almighty with his creatures. God is not erratic but disciplined in his manner of ruling all things. The classical mind recognized a deep continuity between the moral law and the laws of nature.[3] And Christians came to realize that the wise, predictable pattern to the universe (what the Greeks called the Logos) is, in fact, the mind of Christ. When we study math, we glimpse God's wise ordering of the world in his Son.[4] Listen, for example, to Jesus's geometric wisdom in the book of Proverbs, describing how he—as eternal Wisdom itself—worked alongside his Father in the creation of the world:

> When he established the heavens, I was there;
>   when he drew a circle on the face of the deep,
> when he made firm the skies above,
>   when he established the fountains of the deep,
> when he assigned to the sea its limit,
>   so that the waters might not transgress his command,
> when he marked out the foundations of the earth,
>   then I was beside him, like a master workman,
> and I was daily his delight,
>   rejoicing before him always. (Prov 8:27–30)

When I studied math, I had no idea I would eventually become a pastor. But years later, I found that the intellectual rigor, precision, and logical thinking I learned in my classes were fantastic training for sermon writing. Math demands care in language and logic. It requires cutting out anything superfluous to the thing you're pursuing. Math is clean, tight, and focused. Math is the contemplation of God's ordered ways, and such contemplation can only have a wisening effect on a person.

But God's mathematical order is also beautiful and, therefore, beautifying. There is a philosophical debate about whether mathematical truth is something we *discover* or something we *invent*. Is the quadratic formula a deep truth in the universe or a cultural product of René Descartes in the seventeenth century? The answer to this puzzle (like so many other puzzles in human life) is *both*. Math traces the threads of God's thoughts, woven into the very fabric of the earth for us to find. In math, the wisely ordered and subtle mind of the Creator and the earthy inventiveness of scrappy human beings come together in a beautiful marriage.

Such a vision of math studies flies in the face of our modern infatuation with STEM courses. Why do we love training in Science, Technology, Engineering, and Math today? Because students can get good jobs with them, jobs which will make us more rich and powerful as a society. This is understandable; it's truly awe-inspiring to consider the vast applications of mathematics across medicine, technology, and business that have revolutionized our world. It's arguable that no other discipline has been so practically fruitful throughout the centuries. And it's certainly not wrong to want a good job, using math or otherwise. But historically, math was largely cultivated during times of leisure. Royal courts might have sponsored mathematicians because they wanted power and prestige, but mathematicians like astronomer Johannes Kepler were focused on something more sublime:

> I consider it a right, yes, a duty, to search in a cautious manner for the number, sizes and weights, the norms of everything He has created. For these secrets are not of the kind whose research should be forbidden; rather, they are set before our eyes like a mirror so that by examining them we observe to some extent the goodness and wisdom of the Creator.[5]

It wasn't pragmatism but wonder and curiosity that led Isaac Newton to "the Calculus" or Blaise Pascal to lay the foundations of probability theory.

A number of people have told me they loved geometry as a high school student because of its emphasis on proofs. The presentation of proofs to peers on a whiteboard is a point of convergence displaying the two great skills of classical education: language and math. Yet, I didn't return to an emphasis on proof demonstration until my third year of college. Why is that? Mainly because modern math is so pragmatic. We only care about balancing a checkbook or learning engineering and statistics. Math is only there to serve science and business. As a result, the parts of math that many students actually enjoyed have been cut away in an emphasis on what's *useful.*

A classical approach to math resists the pragmatism of contemporary culture. The most valuable things in life aren't about power and wealth: friendship, laughter, play—and, above all, worship. Math is often at its best when it's like laughter—unnecessary but delightful. And just as a life filled with laughter will be one that's generally healthy, a mind trained in math will be one that's generally useful and practical. As I've said throughout this book, begin with love and everything else gets thrown in. "Seek first the kingdom ... and all these things will be added to you" (Matt 6:33). Love math, and you'll end up good at something that likely pays well, but begin with a desire for power or wealth, and you may end up empty. I'm not suggesting we strive for a persnickety perfectionism. I'm describing the care that goes into a craft. A well-trained woodworker would never say, "Who cares if the cabinets are off by a few inches?" Those few inches can disrupt the proportions of the whole kitchen. Mathematical proportion and precision are aesthetic qualities suitable for every craft. Beauty is well-ordered, whether in geometry or architecture or painting.

WAITING ON TRUTH

Simone Weil was a Christian mystic and a brilliant mathematician and philosopher. She considered communion with God and the study of mathematics to be similar experiences:

> Making known to the child or student the special way of "waiting on truth" in every problem, whether in language or mathematics or any other subject, is what Weil identifies as the first duty of a teacher. For this makes it an exercise in "waiting on God," which God will one day reward with tenderness.[6]

Anyone who has studied math knows exactly the experience Weil is describing. You've been staring at the problem thinking, "I have no clue how to do this," when all of a sudden, it dawns on you. Often, I would work all day on a proof, and it wasn't until deep in the night as I slept that the solution would come to me in a dream. Math is for dreamers, mystics, and visionaries.

The attention demanded of us in the study of math is very close to the attention given when we love or desire anything. The Bible reader will often come to a verse that makes no sense to her. She must not ignore this problem by skipping over the verse or by dismissing the Bible as foolish. She must pray, asking God to reveal the truth of the verse. How willingly the Lord does so! I always prayed before math exams, just as I would pray before a devotional time in the Bible: "Open my eyes, that I may behold wondrous things" (Ps 119:18).

Math, likewise, requires patience and trust: Patience for a solution to arise and trust that it *will* eventually arise. The biggest problem for most students is fear blocking their willingness to humbly sit with a problem and wait until the truth reveals itself. Listening to other people involves the same patience and attention. To understand them—to hear when they're beginning to open up to you—takes patience.

This speaks to another vital connection between math and truth. The mathematician loves math when math *has loved him first*. To reveal is an act of love, isn't it? Solving a math problem is work, but it's also a gift because it wasn't possible until truth revealed itself—unearned, undeserved, simply to be received. That is really what it feels like. Just as faithful Christians believe God's goodness will reveal itself in time in our lives, careful mathematicians believe the solution to the problem will reveal itself in time.

This is why we often coach our students not to say, "I don't know how to do this," but "I don't know how to do this *yet*." The young heart needs to learn the patience of waiting for the truth. The ability to wait on truth is one of the most important skills not only for math but for life.

THE NATURAL WORLD

As modern people, it's quite obvious to us that the physical world operates in mathematical patterns. It's hard for us to imagine seeing the world any other way. But a major historical question is: Why was it in Christendom that science finally flourished? Why not in the great Greek or Chinese civilizations, which seemed so close to the same breakthrough?

I've already mentioned one important answer: Most ancient cultures believed matter to be chaotic rather than ruled by the rational, purposeful mind of a Creator. The Greeks believed in the Logos, the orderly structure behind the physical universe. But it was Christians whose gospel said, "The Word [the Logos] became flesh and dwelt among us, and we have seen his glory, glory as of the only Son from the Father, full of grace and truth" (John 1:14). This idea was revolutionary. How could something so pure and unchanging as the eternal Logos become something so unpredictable, decaying, and filled with passions as *flesh*? The Greek mind had set spirit and matter against each other; the study of matter couldn't lead to the deep spiritual truths of the universe.

But Christians (and Jewish believers before us) have always affirmed that God reliably reveals himself in and through the physical world. The creation is the revelation of God's wisdom and power as our Creator (Rom 1:20), just as the physical incarnation of the Son of God is the ultimate revelation of his grace and faithfulness as our Savior.

Science is about observing, touching, hearing, measuring the physical creation, and, through this physical experience, forming theories that try to best explain the data. This scientific activity of studying the natural world around us is what humans were first called to do in the garden. Adam and Eve were commanded to exercise dominion over the creation through naming the creatures (Gen 1:28; 2:19–20). Science is how we name the physical world, thereby exercising dominion over it. Solomon's example shows us that such identification and classification takes deep wisdom:

> He spoke of trees, from the cedar that is in Lebanon to the hyssop that grows out of the wall. He spoke also of beasts, and of birds, and of reptiles, and of fish. And people of all nations came to hear the wisdom of Solomon, and from all the kings of the earth, who had heard of his wisdom. (1 Kgs 4:33–34)

The apostle John even described coming to know the gospel in a way that sounds close to scientific experimentation:

> That which was from the beginning, which we have heard, which we have seen with our eyes, which we looked upon and have touched with our hands, concerning the word of life. (1 John 1:1)

John's good news, of course, isn't a theory about God. Truth with a capital T revealed himself directly to John.

Any theory can always be replaced by a better one—and good scientists welcome this—because they know careful study can never exhaust the natural world of riches yet to be discovered. No single theory can be the Truth in some final, unquestionable sense but only a useful approximation of the deep reality of the world God has made. The church wasn't suspicious of Galileo because he offered a new model of the solar system (the authorities hadn't challenged Copernicus in the same way a century earlier). They challenged him because he wanted his new theory to be elevated to the unquestionable status of Truth.[7]

How do these beliefs about the natural world as created by God and studied by science shape the classical school? It means that science should be hands-on, experimental, observational, and physical. Science class is a tremendous opportunity for classical schools to avoid being overly esoteric and intellectual. Students should build rockets, burn things, and get their hands dirty. Any chance to not simply diagram a physics or chemistry problem but to experience it is preferable. (We had a student who killed a coyote on his family's property, and the science teacher rushed over to prepare it to be dissected by the students the next day!) The impulse to touch the physical world and experience it should be the mark of classical school science.

All of this trains the young mind in empiricism: What does the empirical data actually say? Increasingly, our culture believes things because of how they serve our ideologies and not because they have been confirmed through experimentation and reason. Being willing to observe data and accept what it says is an act of humility. In the thirteenth century, Christian theologian and philosopher Thomas Aquinas helped to lay the foundation for the scientific discoveries in the centuries after him. Chesterton says this about Aquinas:

> St. Thomas had the scientific humility in this very vivid and special sense: that he was ready to take the lowest place; for the examination of the lowest things. ... He was willing to begin to study the reality of the world in the reality of the worm. ... The study of the humblest fact will lead to the study of the highest truths.[8]

The earthiness of the scientific method—with its insistence on empirical observation and the reiteration of trial and error—has been essential for training the Christian mind in a humble, inquisitive posture toward the natural world.

SCIENCE AND FAITH

But naturally, this raises the question, "What happens when scientific observation contradicts Christian faith?" Whenever we ask this, we must always remember that the only reason science can make any truth claims at all is because it's premised on the assumption of a world governed by the Bible's sovereign God of creation and providence. As I said earlier, pre-Christian cultures didn't have these assumptions about the world that have led to such a flourishing of science. Only the Bible teaches an unchanging God who governs the world through "laws of nature." The God of the Bible loves wisdom and order, and it is the consistency of his character that makes nature intelligible. Theologian Vern Poythress has pointed out that not only science and math but even reason itself are inconceivable apart from the reality of the God whose character they mirror.

> Scientists must believe in God, because scientific laws, by their very definition, bear divine attributes. Scientific laws are omnipotent and universal, personal in character (that is, rational and communicable in language),

> incomprehensible, good, beautiful, just, even Trinitarian, in a sense.[9]

This truth about God is why we believe that science can predict the truth that (for example) the way a physical object behaves today will be the same tomorrow under the same conditions. Since God makes science possible, scientific reasoning should always be understood as "faith seeking understanding" (as Anselm famously put it), not "reason establishing faith."

Though real contradictions between the claims of science and faith are very few, the one that looms large in the minds of many modern people is the conflict between Genesis and Darwin. Though Darwinian evolution is such a small piece of the overall scientific project, it's a central cog in the modern secular rejection of Christianity. As atheist Richard Dawkins put it, "Darwin made it possible to be an intellectually fulfilled atheist."[10] Because of the cultural importance of Darwinism, it is worth addressing it briefly here.

EVOLUTION AS A SCIENTIFIC MODEL

Darwinism speaks to two scientific (and biblical) questions that should be carefully distinguished: How old is the earth? And how did the diversity of life come into being? I don't want to spend much time on the former question. I personally hold a young earth position.[11] The Scriptures simply don't give us much information on this matter. "He has made everything beautiful in its time. Also, he has put eternity into man's heart, yet so that he cannot find out what God has done from the beginning to the end" (Eccl 3:11). Just as the end of history is mysterious to us, so is the beginning.[12] I believe this should be a matter for charitable debate within classical Christian schools; many who uphold the inerrancy of the Scriptures have disagreed on this question.[13] Even Augustine said about the Genesis account, "Let each one, then, take it as he pleases; for it is so profound a passage, that it may well suggest, for the exercise of the reader's tact, many opinions, and none of them widely departing from the rule of faith."[14]

As to the second question about the origin of life and its diversity, many Christians say they believe in a kind of evolution directed by God. If this means that over long ages God by his creative power created the diversity of life on our planet, then we should also leave space for this position to be discussed and debated within classical Christian schools.

But just as with the age of the earth or any other scientific claims, we must refuse to tie our biblical and theological views to any given scientific model—one that will inevitably change over the course of time as more discoveries are made. Therefore, in the case of evolution *as a model for explaining the mechanisms for life's origins and diversity*, I urge teachers, students, and parents to first appreciate the substantial (I would say devastating) flaws in the model itself. But more broadly, all Christians should recognize the atheistic, materialistic worldview underlying Darwinism—the modern myth of evolution, an epic story of godless origins—that we must soundly reject. Not only does the Bible clearly tell us that God made plants and animals "according to their kinds" and that our first parents were his special, direct creation, but as time goes on, an evolutionary theory of origins is increasingly becoming philosophically, mathematically, and empirically absurd.

So first, what are the evidential problems with the evolutionary model? Without space here for a lengthy discussion, I'll just highlight a few glaring evidential issues that have been pointed out:

+ Evolution assumes but doesn't demonstrate that the miraculous series of mutations necessary to form a human eye (or brain or kidney or lung) could emerge by chance, from utter simplicity to unimaginable complexity, so long as there is a sufficiently vast scale of time.

But where's the evidence that adaptive mutations work in such a remarkable way and lead to such astonishing results?[15] I recently read Jerry Coyne's *Why Evolution Is True*, for example, and found this fundamental building block of the theory completely ignored.[16] In mathematics, they call this kind of reasoning hand-waving: when someone skips a key step in a proof, gestures quickly in the hopes that you accept it anyway (" ... and something happens over here ... "), and then moves on. That unproven step is usually the most important part of the whole proof. Evolution often does this. Because of such hand-waving, Christians must appreciate that Darwinism as a scientific explanatory model demonstrates far less than it claims.

+ Evolution assumes the existence of reproductive life from the beginning. It needs a reproducing cell to start the long chain of life that must follow. But evolution cannot account for life's initial origin and has no evidence of life arising spontaneously from non-life.

+ Evolution has claimed for 150 years to rely on the evidence of a fossil record showing gradual changes between species over eons. Now, after over a century of digging up bones, that fossil record simply hasn't materialized. Fossils are clumped by time and kind, and even if the earth is very old, the appearance of new species generally happens suddenly in biological "explosions." As Harvard paleontologist Stephen Jay Gould writes, "But earth scorns our simplifications, and becomes much more interesting in its derision. The history of life is not a continuum of development, but a record punctuated by brief—sometimes geologically instantaneous—episodes of mass extinction and subsequent diversification."[17]

+ Evolution cannot account for the evidence of *irreducible complexity*—that is, integrated biological functions that are only advantageous if each part of a complex system evolved simultaneously. Even the first life form would require incredible complexities for which evolution cannot account. Darwin, who believed cells were more like simple blobs of matter, would likely not have invented his theory at all if he had our contemporary evidence of the complexity of even a single living cell.
+ Evolution is statistically impossible. The amount of time required for random mutations to develop the incalculable number of complex biological functions in living creatures is far larger than even the oldest estimates of the universe.[18]

These are only some of the evidential problems with the theory; I haven't even touched on the philosophical problems. Evolution, for example, cannot account for the existence of consciousness itself. How can purposeful, personal beings arise from an impersonal and purposeless process? Even atheist philosophers have struggled with the impossibility of consciousness arising from a closed materialistic system.[19]

So, if evolution isn't true, what is the true history of life on our planet? We must be humble enough to say, "There's a lot we don't know." Though the Bible's account is without error, it's by no means a complete record of biological life. By faith we do science, believing that the same God who authored the Scriptures is the God who rules nature with truth and wisdom and power and order. God cannot lie; God cannot contradict himself. As we grow in wisdom, we will find again and again that all things hold together in Jesus.

EVOLUTION AS A SECULAR MYTH

If evolution has such scientific problems, why is it so fiercely defended by so many scientists? Well, that is the second matter—the deeper issue surrounding evolution as a *worldview*. Closely tied to the scientific investigation around origins is the myth of evolutionism. C. S. Lewis has described evolution as possibly the greatest (and most tragic) myth ever devised by the human heart. At its center is man's hubris—our ambition and pride. Against all odds, though we were once just microscopic amoeba in a vast, hostile ocean—"at first everything seems to be against the infant hero of our drama"—through our persistent will to survive, the strongest and most beautiful among us, the fittest, conquered against all odds, until we rose up to rule the world as rational modern man.[20]

The story of evolution is that man raises himself up to become a god—but in the end, he will tragically disappear into the blackness of an eternal night. He ascends from almost nothing but ultimately descends into absolutely nothing.

The reason this myth ultimately fails as an explanation for life is because it's the exact inversion of the gospel. Instead of man raising himself up—evolving—from the lowest place, in the gospel, God himself came down to the lowest place. Man was not strong but weak. Man was not noble but wretched. He could not raise himself up—but was debasing himself deeper and deeper into darkness. But by grace, the Son of God descended to the lowest place (Eph 4:9–10)—he even became a zygote in the womb of his mother, like an amoeba. He did not select the fittest (1 Cor 1:26) but those who knew how unfit they were, that he might raise us out of the meaningless darkness (1 Pet 2:9) into the beauty and vitality of life eternal.

These two stories are irreconcilably at odds. One is about the glory of man; the other the glory of God that he then shares with sinners by grace. One is a tragedy; the other a comedy. One empties life of any ultimate meaning; the other fills heaven and earth with the goodness, beauty, and truth of the Son of God.

Here again, we see how all things hold together in Jesus and that the deep reality of the universe is found only in his love. Evolution is emphatically not a story of love. It is a story of competition, making the world into a brutal machine of human pride and power.

Besides being tragic, Lewis points out that this myth is ultimately self-defeating:

> The content of the Myth thus knocks from under me the only ground on which I could possibly believe the Myth to be true. If my own mind is a product of the irrational—if what seem my clearest reasonings are only the way in which a creature conditioned as I am is bound to feel—how shall I trust my mind when it tells me about Evolution?[21]

So, the faithful classical Christian school must always remember that science will never grant us faith. But thoughtful, well-reasoned faith will always lead us into sound science. It will lead us into the orderly and beautiful way the sovereign God rules his creatures. So, we don't let science question the Bible or the objects of Christian orthodoxy because these deep assumptions about the world are the very foundation on which science is built.

Next to the Word of God, music deserves the highest praise. … For whether to comfort the sad, to terrify the happy, to encourage the despairing, to humble the proud, to calm the passionate, or to appease those full of hate—and who could number all these masts of the human heart, namely, the emotions, inclinations, and affections that impel men to evil or good?—what more effective means than music could you find?

Martin Luther, *Works*

10

SINGING

The goal of human life is to glorify God and enjoy him forever, and what embodies this ultimate purpose better than singing? Christian worship closes with the doxology, and the Christian life culminates in endless praise to God. We were made to sing. And so it is fitting that this book ends with a chapter on song.

Singing ties together many of the themes we've covered in this book. We sing about God's covenant promises and his grace. Singing is the backbone of the liturgy of the day. Nothing strengthens a Grammar student's memory like singing. Nothing ties together the beauty, goodness,and truth of the gospel like a beautiful song coming from the heart of one of God's children. Gospel education is filled with song.

The argument of this book has been that the goal of education is the formation of a child in love through the gospel. Throughout history, Christians have seen the liberal arts and classical learning as the most powerful vehicle and the most suitable method for just this kind of love-forming, gospel-centered education.

As we come to our final chapter, this vision of education comes to a point as we see the importance of singing in a Christian school. The background sounds of a gospel school are children singing and chanting. In the Grammar School, they'll sing the memory of the human race into their minds. In the Logic and Rhetoric Schools, they will sing the beauty and subtlety of divine and human truth into their souls. In fact, the Bible tells us that singing and learning are closely tied together:

> Let the word of Christ dwell in you richly, teaching and admonishing one another in all wisdom, singing psalms and hymns and spiritual songs, with thankfulness in your hearts to God. (Col 3:16)

Singing should be as natural an outflow of believing, grateful hearts as praying is. But also, Paul says, it's one of the main ways we teach and encourage each other.

So many Christians today fail to appreciate that learning to sing is one of the most essential skills for being a disciple of Jesus. Many Christians don't even sing in church and assume that this is no big deal because they don't know how to do it. We think what matters is what is in my heart, and so it doesn't really matter how that is expressed with my body. But how can you live a life of praise to God if you don't know how to sing, or you aren't confident enough to open your mouth in worship? Martin Luther said that after biblical teaching, the most important skill for a pastor is being able to sing well. It is that essential to the Christian life. But why?

St. Augustine wrote a book on music, whose final section is about how music shapes the deepest affections in a person's heart. Augustine had experienced this himself. He was a teacher of rhetoric in Milan and was converted under the ministry of the bishop Ambrose. After his baptism, he said that the dread over his former life faded from his mind, and his heart was renewed:

> How copiously I wept at your hymns and canticles, how intensely was I moved by the lovely harmonies of your singing Church! Those voices flooded my ears, and the truth was distilled into my heart until it overflowed in loving devotion; my tears ran down, and I was the better for them.[1]

What Augustine tells us here is that the Holy Spirit uses music to form our deepest desires—and we are the better for it. Maybe no other earthly thing has the power to move our affections and our desires like music. I have had elderly congregants who no longer knew the names of their own children but who could still sing "Be Still My Soul" because it had been woven into their memory through years of worship. If there is one thing that God created to shape the desires, affections, and emotions of human beings, it is music.

An education that forms children in love will have singing not on the margins but in the center. Teachers might need to learn to sing with joy and passion—like they mean it. And above all, the music teacher must be one who inspires the culture of the school around song. She's not just a great musician herself, but she chooses settings achievable for young voices, while also stretching the students into musical heights they never thought they could reach.

SINGING IN PARTS (HARMONIZING)

The gospel tells us that the one true and living God exists in three persons. Within God himself, there is unity and diversity. This mystery is revealed in the person of Christ, who tells us, "I am in the Father and the Father is in me. ... In that day you will know that I am in my Father, and you in me, and I in you" (John 14:11, 20). Mutual indwelling is the nature of God himself and, therefore, the nature of our life in God.

This one-in-three, mutual indwelling quality can be found woven into everything God has made. One of the most beautiful places is in the musical chord. Three distinct sounds, each occupying the same space, dwell within each other. They don't compete with each other, but they harmonize and enhance each other, making each other into something more rich and more beautiful than if they had been alone. Even the tension of minors and diminished chords that cry out for resolution are a small glimmer of how Jesus has assumed our sin on the cross, crying out, "My God, my God, why have you forsaken me?" Though always in perfect harmony with his Father, he has taken into his person all the unresolved tensions of the created order and resolved them in the harmony of his sovereign conducting of all things according to his perfect composition.

"Music envelops you," observes theologian Peter J. Leithart. "It totally surrounds you in every bit of the space of the room, but it doesn't imprison you."[2] There are few experiences in life that feel more like being "in God" than when your voice is immersed in the choir of God's people, singing powerfully and beautifully in parts. The Bible seems to suggest this, for the Lord is "enthroned on the praises of Israel" (Ps 22:3). God dwells in the songs of his people.

Anyone who has done this will know that singing well in parts involves blending voices. Each singer must listen to and be sensitive to the voices and vibrations of the others as the whole group strives to match their frequencies to one another. When they succeed, the singers experience a profound pleasure that can only be called beautiful, good, and true. In a similar way, a life of love learns to hear others and tries to match and complement their frequencies. How could such an experience not be a training in love?

For those who don't know how to harmonize, it is easy to dismiss the skill with, "I am tone deaf. I literally can't hold a tune." I personally think being "tone deaf" is rare. Harmonizing certainly comes easier for some than others (just like any other skill). But the skill no doubt comes easier if the building blocks are put in place from the earlier grades. As our school has matured, it is clear that kids whose training started earlier were capable of much more by the time they hit the logic and rhetoric stages.

Singing is not only about harmonizing with other human beings but about harmonizing with all of nature itself. The Bible often talks of all creatures joining in chorus to praise God. The classical Christian mind has for centuries viewed the cycles of the seasons and the movements of the stars to be the rhythmic dance of God's creation. As humans learn to sing in harmony, their souls are trained to resonate with the wisdom of nature, and we join the song that began at the creation, "when the morning stars sang together and all the sons of God shouted for joy" (Job 38:7).

THE BODY IS AN INSTRUMENT

The human body is the greatest instrument in the world. When it is tuned and played rightly, nothing can touch the heart or transcend the soul like it. Not only are its tones rich and subtle, but the rational mind can join words and stories to sounds, rhythms, and melodies that resonate with the emotions.

All children were gifted one of these instruments by God, and he intends for them to use it. But just like learning any other instrument, children need technique, practice, and musical knowledge. They need to learn to breathe, relax their face, open their mouths, and push out their belly buttons. Their eyes should be bright and open.

One of the joys of singing is how bodily it is. We mentioned earlier that the classical school must resist the temptation to neglect the body in favor of the mind. One way to do this is to make singing a daily part of the daily routine. Singing engages diaphragm and lungs, mouth, face, tongue, shoulders—even how you stand. When done right, the song reverberates through every fiber of a person's being. Singing is often best taught when students are marched around, forced to engage their whole bodies.

When we sing, it is not only our own bodies that vibrate, but the bodies of those around us begin to vibrate at the same frequency. This is why the human voice is so intimate. An education in love is giving children the skill in emotional and spiritual intimacy.

The relationship between song and body is remarkable: Singing takes truths and reverberates them through our whole being—bones, nerves, muscles, blood. The truth literally becomes the frequency of the person's body. We intuitively sense that there is some relationship between this reverberation and the working of the Holy Spirit. We feel music in our bodies and say, "God's Spirit was moving in me." Some dismiss this as being sentimental. But if the words being sung are theological truths, the Scriptures disagree. When the apostle Paul describes a person filled with the Holy Spirit, four of the five verbs he uses involve singing:

> Be filled with the Spirit, addressing one another in psalms and hymns and spiritual songs, singing and making melody to the Lord with your heart, giving thanks always and for everything to God the Father in the name of our Lord

> Jesus Christ, submitting to one another out of reverence for Christ. (Eph 5:18–21)

Our bodies are instruments designed by God to express truth in song. A body filled with the Holy Spirit is a body that sings.

Though classical schools should encourage learning all kinds of musical instruments, singing is as basic and essential as reading and math.

MUSICAL KNOWLEDGE

Another reason to emphasize singing is because it is a skill that students will use throughout their lives. The most important hour of a Christian's week is the one spent gathered with God's people in worship on the Lord's Day, singing God's praise. A gospel culture will then bring song from the sanctuary into the home, around the dinner table with family and friends. Singing may even prove to be the skill most comforting when they come to their death beds. Though all students have been given a beautiful wind instrument in their bodies that they must learn to play, singing also gives foundational knowledge of music theory. The ability to see notes on a page and quickly sing along or harmonize is a tremendous gift. Many piano teachers will note the value singing adds to playing piano. The ability to sing scores of songs helps the musical intuition, and by the time a student is in fourth grade, he is familiar with basics like the pentatonic scale. By the end of the Grammar School, children can sight read basic melodies, just as they can sound out most difficult words in a book they are reading.

The singing of Logic students begins to stretch them in the same ways their humanities discussions will become more challenging and deep. Rounds that they had learned in Grammar School begin to translate into harmonizing, using thirds and fifths they might not have even realized they were singing in those earlier songs. The Quadrivium sees music as a mathematical subject, and so students will know how to write notation and understand different time signatures. These will give them the tools in the later years to compose their own pieces of music. We believe that, even if they don't grow up to become composers, musical knowledge should be basic to every Christian.

But more importantly, a few magical experiences of layered singing, especially when successfully performed for others, have the ability to ignite a desire to sing more and more challenging pieces of music. There is hardly any pleasure like it in the world, when, with their friends, a student nails a harmony that stretches them to the limits of their capabilities. This is the goal at the logic stage: to form in the students a hunger for deeper, complex, and beautiful music—when the teacher asks, "Do you think we can do this?" for students to confidently say, "Yes!"

Such experiences will also certainly broaden their musical appreciation. Though most young people consume swaths of pop music, it is a shame if they have no appetite beyond that. It is okay to have a liking for both Skittles and a fine Pinot Noir, but it would be a shame if you only liked Skittles. We want our children to be able to enjoy the full spectrum of God-given pleasure. Pop music is designed to be quickly liked, consumed, and discarded. That doesn't mean it is bad. It just means children don't need a teacher to help them love Taylor Swift but might need a teacher to help them love Palestrina.

MUSIC AND THE NUMINOUS

This leads to music in the Rhetoric school, which is largely focused on performance. One of the primary goals of the choir curriculum is to actually bless the parents and friends who come to concerts and spring programs. These gatherings are not meant to mainly let the students show off or for grandparents to congratulate the hard work of their students. These are times to serve those who come—to use the skills they've learned to give their guests an experience of transcendence. C. S. Lewis wrote about how modern art has changed from serving the recipient to serving the artist.[3] Art (nowadays) is about the self-expression of the artist. We no longer criticize the artist for his shoddy artwork but criticize the observer of the art for not being sophisticated enough to appreciate it. This is not a Christian view of art as an act of love.[4]

The "rhetoric" of the high school choir is meant to stir the hearts of the school's broader community to encounter and wonder at the goodness of Christ. We want those who come to have an experience of the numinous—the sense that this world is not just a dead mass of atoms and forces but that there is a spiritual Presence that haunts the marvels of the creation. Modern culture has been disenchanted and lost its wonder of the symbolic meaning of the cosmos and the glory and meaning that charges everything around us. The songs of the classical student are meant to help us recapture the imaginative wonder of this mythological world in which you and I are creatures. There is a deep beauty behind the mountains and the stars. We long to be united to that beauty, and humans, as those who are made in the likeness of that beauty, have the calling to lead others to it.

BEING HUMAN

Music, along with the other arts, has been historically considered integral to the humanities, studied by humanists. They have this name because they are meant to help us become more human. Being human means loving, feeling, thinking, listening, enjoying, serving, repenting, and singing. All of these require a subtle and careful wisdom.

But what is a human? The Bible says a human is a creature made after the image of God. A human is not the image of God but made after his image. So what then is God's image? Colossians 1:13, 15 tells us: "He has delivered us from the domain of darkness and transferred us to the kingdom of his beloved Son. ... He is the image of the invisible God."

When the humanities—when the singing of the deep beauty of existence—make our hearts and minds more human, what they are actually doing is making us like Christ. Our children are God's artwork. He is the potter; they are the clay. He is the sculptor; they are the statues. They are not dead statues made of marble. They are living statues—speaking, loving, running, playing, praying, debating, thinking, and singing—statues. The classical Christian school is an Artist's studio, and his medium is flesh and blood, soul and mind. His tools are the Word of God and wisdom of the ages.

May he send out into the world thousands upon thousands of these beautiful, unique works of art. And the pattern our Lord is following, in forming with love each one, is Beauty, Goodness, and Truth himself—the image of God, the true man, Jesus Christ. So we end this chapter, and this book, where all things will end:

> *Let everything that has breath praise the Lord!* (Psalm 150:6)

NINE THESES OF GOSPEL EDUCATION

JESUS IS THE GREATEST TEACHER in history. That's why this book is not so much a how-to manual for running a Christian school, but a manifesto envisioning a type of education that is distinctly generated by the gospel of Jesus Christ. Christianity has been the most culturally generative power in human history, and it will continue to produce new cultural fruit from now until the consummation of all things. For people who love the gospel of Jesus Christ, this cultural fruit from generations past will be a treasured inheritance that they will want to ensure has been entrusted to their children as well as to generations that follow after them. Gospel education passes along this culture. These nine theses summarize the key convictions underlying this vision of gospel education.

1. Because Jesus is a King building a civilization on the earth, gospel education is a key way children are enculturated into the ways of his culture.

2. Because Jesus's civilization is defined by love, gospel education forms God's covenant love in children through a gospel culture and a liturgical pattern to the school day.

3. Because Jesus is King over heaven and earth, gospel education integrates all subjects into a coherent worldview.

4. Because Jesus has been enculturating humans in his truth, goodness, and beauty for many centuries, gospel education builds on the historic Christian pedagogy of the seven liberal arts: grammar, logic, and rhetoric (the Trivium); and arithmetic, geometry, science, and music (the Quadrivium).

5. Because Jesus is not only King but also the eternal Word of God, gospel Grammar students learn to read and write and begin to memorize the basic knowledge of Christian civilization.

6. Because Jesus is the true Word who holds all things together, gospel Logic students learn through the primary sources how Christ connects history into a unified story and how the paradoxes of Christ are at the center of the Great Conversation of human civilization.

7. Because Jesus's Word is good news to a lost world, gospel Rhetoric students learn to contemplate deeply the ways of Christ that they might persuade others of his truth and poetically communicate his goodness and beauty.

8. Because Jesus is the word of all creation, gospel math is an exploration of the orderly wisdom of Christ that has been revealed in the physical world studied by science.

9. Because Jesus alone satisfies the deepest desire of the human heart as both Lord and Savior, gospel singing tunes the hearts and the bodies of students to long for his love and to seek his kingdom.

NINE THESES EXPLAINED

1. Because Jesus is a King building a civilization on the earth, gospel education is a key way children are enculturated into the ways of his society.

The Bible tells us that Jesus's purpose for world history is to build a civilization in which he is honored. Another way to say this is that the heavenly city (where God's will is done perfectly) is becoming not just a city in heaven, but also on the earth. Cities are places of rich human culture. So if Christianity is about Jesus building a city on the earth, Christianity is a culture. It doesn't simply fight culture or even transform culture. It has its own culture, its own stories and art and traditions and practices. It has its own understanding of history and definition of the meaning of life. It is able to both understand and challenge every human culture.

Education then is about enculturating Christian children into the civilization that Jesus has been building for 2,000 years and is continuing to build in our day. And the central tenet of the culture Jesus is building is love. The two greatest commandments of our King's will is that we love God and love our neighbor. That means if education is about enculturating Christian children into the traditions of the City of God, then education is about Jesus forming his love into the children of his people. And that is the primary thesis of this book.

2. Because Jesus's civilization is defined by love, gospel education forms God's covenant love in children through a gospel culture and a liturgical pattern to the school day.

The goal of education is ultimately about forming the love of Christ in each student. Every school has an ideal image toward which they are forming their students—the ideal graduate. For us, Jesus is the ideal human, the embodiment of love, toward whom students ought to be shaped. The school exists for forming the hearts, minds, and behaviors of Christian children into the image of Christ.

Being formed in Christ's love begins when God places his strong and loving arms around the children of his people and says, "Within these arms, you will grow to think and feel and speak and act and laugh. Because I have first loved you, you too will learn to love." The Bible's word for God's nurturing and protecting embrace is covenant. God's covenant promises to our children are the foundation of a Christian school and the basis for our children's education and discipleship.

God's covenant love also creates a kind of culture in the school, marked by the gospel principle: "We love because he first loved us" (1 John 4:19). In a gospel school, this principle permeates not only the teaching and chapel talks but the very way the community relates to one another among faculty, staff, students, and parents. Gospel-fueled love should be the mood of the school; you should sense it as soon as you spend even a day there.

A gospel mentality deeply shapes how rules are used in the school as well. Rules are meant to lead children to Christ. The rules reveal the sins of the students, creating opportunities for them to experience repentance and faith. The rules strike fear in bullies who would disrupt the culture of grace and love. The rules also train students in godly manners which are learned, embodied acts of love.

So formation in love happens through God's covenant in a gospel culture, but also through the carefully ordered liturgy of the day—a school day structured around the spiritual disciplines—Scripture and catechesis, prayer and song, work and meals, and even the uniforms the students wear. While the gospel changes a child from the inside out, these spiritual habits shape and direct that new heart from the outside-in, to love God and his kingdom in deeper and deeper ways.

3. Because Jesus is King over heaven and earth, gospel education integrates all subjects into a coherent worldview.

Whether we know it or not, every one of us brings foundational assumptions to our understanding of the world. These assumptions shape the way we approach everything, including learning and teaching. No education is neutral. These assumptions (whether Christian or not) are always built on faith and are called a worldview. The center of the Christian worldview is the person of Jesus Christ who gives us eyes to understand rightly everything he has made. There is no area of life or knowledge left untouched by the Christian worldview. It's an amazingly coherent and comprehensive framework for understanding God, his world, and humanity.

A coherent and comprehensive worldview is essential for students to become people of wisdom. Gospel education trains students in wisdom by integrating the various disciplines of knowledge, striving to tie together the many parts of learning that often get separated: literature and history, Bible and science, math and writing, and so on. An integrated education resists the fracturing of knowledge into separate subjects, constantly striving to discern how the various things we learn fit into a consistent whole. "In [Christ] all things hold together" (Col 1:17). He is the organizing principle of reality. The wise person sees how everything is connected in Jesus.

Training in Christian wisdom brings wholeness and coherence to the soul by integrating all the areas of learning in Christ himself. He is the Lawgiver behind the laws of nature; he is the Author of the story of history; he is the Artist who invented color, form, and subtlety; he is the Goodness at the heart of morality; he is the Hero of the Bible; he is the Word from whom language is derived; he dwells in the triune community of which human society is a reflection. Life makes sense in Jesus.

The most important way for a school to achieve this integration is through teachers who themselves are a living curriculum. Within their own minds, all things have begun to hold together in Jesus. Their wide-ranging curiosities have led them to make connections in God's wild and diverse world. They see that Jesus is the answer to the world's riddles a thousand ways over. One example of how our school practices this integration is through the humanities block, a single course that ties together literature, history, theology, geography, writing, speech, and debate all into a unified study of primary sources.

4. Because Jesus has been enculturating humans in his truth, goodness, and beauty for many centuries, gospel education builds on the historic Christian pedagogy of the seven liberal arts: grammar, logic, and rhetoric (the Trivium), and arithmetic, geometry, science, and music (the Quadrivium).

Historically, one dominant Christian strategy for shaping young people in the love and wisdom of Christ is the seven liberal arts. These arts are divided into two classes: the Trivium (grammar, logic, and rhetoric) and the Quadrivium (arithmetic, geometry, astronomy, and music). The Trivium focuses on language skills and the Quadrivium on mathematical skills.

The liberal arts are meant to empower students by training them in the classical subjects and methods best suited to cultivating people who are truly free. According to the Bible, a person is truly free when he has submitted himself to the truth of God's word. As our Lord says, "the truth will set you free" (John 8:32). As students read and discuss the great theologians and dreamers and philosophers and moralists and poets whose writings helped build Christendom, they join the Great Conversation of the Western world and ask for themselves the deep questions of life, death, God, justice, and human society.

The Trivium gives children the cultural knowledge to join the Great Conversation of Western civilization (grammar), the logical precision to discern truth from error (logic), and the grace to speak and write with subtlety, conviction, and persuasiveness (rhetoric). Every student begins in Grammar School learning not only to read and write, but memorizing the dates, places, names, capitals, battles, parts of speech, animal species, poems, math facts, and so on. Through chants and songs, a wealth of facts can be absorbed efficiently by an elementary school student. Once he hits (roughly) seventh grade, however, he wants to start debating what he's learned—it's time for training in logic (especially since he's going to find himself committing all kinds of fallacies!). The high school years then polish the crude argument of the middle schooler into the persuasive and poetical speech of the rhetorician.

The Quadrivium is also woven throughout the education. Gospel schools put special emphasis on a love of math and work to have science that is as interactive with the physical world as possible. Lastly, and maybe most significantly, gospel schools are filled with singing—not just as a marginal subject, but required for every student—that is woven through every stage of learning.

5. Because Jesus is not only King but also the eternal Word of God, gospel Grammar students learn to read and write and begin to memorize the basic knowledge of Christian civilization.

The first stage of a classical education is called the Grammar School (grades K–6), granting children the awe-inspiring powers of reading, memorization, and writing.

Reading is the first thing humanity needs to learn in order to know the love of Christ, as he has been revealed to us in a book, the Bible. We can only know God from reading or being read to. Gospel classical schools must excel at teaching students to read well, infusing a deep love of reading from the earliest ages. We start with the reliable methods of phonics in kindergarten and first grade. All year, every day, at every level, reading is assigned. It's best that the reading is varied. Rotate short and long books, breezy and thick. Provide fun reads the kids naturally enjoy and others that stretch and shape their literary tastes. Read poems. Read science. Of course, read God's Word daily.

Because true literacy requires far more than just phonics, Dorothy Sayers broadened the Grammar School to encompass not only learning to read and write but learning the grammar of every subject.[1] There are basic facts belonging to every subject from history to anatomy to geography to language. Dates, capitals, presidents, battles, parts of speech, bits of poetry—these are the grammatical building blocks of an education. They all must become readily available to the mind of a young student. And these can only be acquired by extensive memorization. The best way to memorize is through songs and chants, so always in the background of such a school, at any hour of the day, you'll hear children singing. Singing praise to God. Singing the presidents of the United States or the countries of Africa. Singing the different kinds of animals that live in water. The goal of memorization is to give a child a memory. When children memorize the basic knowledge acquired by human culture, they are inheriting the collective memory of Jesus's civilization.

Grammar is an art or a skill and, mainly, the skill of using words. Young people can learn this art and become great with words, but we must give them the fundamental techniques if they are going to do it well. Just as the Grammar student must read, read, read, and memorize, memorize, memorize, so they must write, write, write. Every day and every week, they will write something. In the Grammar School, they're given the skills of using adjectives, relative clauses, and adverbs. Over thirteen years of primary and secondary schooling, they will write pages of essays, book reviews, creative pieces, and persuasive papers. Through this repeated action, the great skill of writing becomes more and more natural.

6. Because Jesus as the true Word holds all things together, gospel Logic students learn through the primary sources of the Western canon how Christ connects history into a unified story and how the paradoxes of Christ are at the center of the Great Conversation of human civilization.

As they move from the Grammar School to the Logic School (grades 7–8), they are transforming from parrots and chanters into young philosophers. Because all things in history and creation hold together in Jesus Christ, the Logic School is about learning to make those connections. It's not as if they ever fully leave grammar behind or that they have never encountered logic before. But the Logic School represents a real change nonetheless—not only in the students' readiness but also in their teachers' emphases and approach. Conversation is the heart of the Logic School. Therefore, the culture of the Logic School is different from that of the Grammar School. The structure is loosened, but the demand to think deeper is heightened.

The backbone of the Logic School conversation is history. Christians understand history to be the great drama which was first summarized in the cryptic words of the Lord to the serpent in Genesis 3:15—"I will put enmity between you and the woman, and between your offspring and her offspring; he shall bruise your head, and you shall bruise his heel." The Bible says that the story of human history is how all the families of the earth, though they have turned from God in rebellion, will nonetheless find blessing in Abraham's seed. "I will bless those who bless you, and him who dishonors you I will curse, and in you all the families of the earth shall be blessed" (Gen 12:3). Students who have been given the mind of Christ will understand history as the unfolding of these promises.

Ultimately, history is vital to Christian formation in love because history is about the Son of God bringing his love to a broken, dark, and sinful world. We're living in a love story! In the Grammar School, students memorize historical dates and names and anecdotes. In the Logic School, they begin to discuss how all these events fit together in the epic tale of the kingdom. How does a student learn to put these pieces together properly?

The Logic School turns each classroom into an incubator for reasoning, discussion, and debate, like a miniature parliament or even a small society. These young philosophers must begin to form opinions and attempt to defend them. As students begin to engage the complexity of God's world, they will begin to see the repeated pattern that God and his way are always paradoxical. God is one being in three persons. Jesus is fully God and fully man. God controls every detail of every moment of his creation, and yet, humans are not robots but responsible for our actions and free to act according to our desires. All fundamental theological beliefs in the Bible are paradoxical.

Such paradoxes don't just appear in theology but in all of life. Every ethical question in life stands at the center of two opposite errors. The study of these paradoxes in the Logic School is called dialectic. The Logic School teacher will regularly divide the class into the two sides of the paradox—creating an apparent conflict—and a great conversation emerges. These conversations help students to learn the essential skill of navigating the world's paradoxical truths. Over and over again, they will find how the solution to these riddles is only found in the person of Jesus Christ. Freedom and discipline. Grace and truth. Compassion and responsibility. Suffering and blessing.

The liberal arts curriculum is built around primary sources. There are many benefits to this. The main benefit is that by reading primary sources students enter into the Great Conversation that human beings have been having for thousands of years about who we are and how we should live. In this way, gospel education is structured around the deepest and most lasting questions of life: What is morality? What is freedom? How much power should a government have? Who is God?

7. Because Jesus's Word is good news to a lost world, gospel Rhetoric students learn to contemplate deeply the ways of Christ that they might persuade others of

> his truth and poetically communicate his goodness and beauty.

If Christian students are to be Christ's witnesses carrying his grace and wisdom into every part of their lives, they must learn to communicate with clarity, humility, and conviction. They must be confident and warm, winsome and compelling, their thoughts presented with both order and beauty.

After the spiritual formation of a student, therefore, rhetoric is the second highest goal of a gospel-centered classical education. Because rhetoric is one of the highest goals in classical learning, the final stage of secondary education (high school) is often referred to as the Rhetoric School (grades 9–12). Just as the Grammar School involves some logic training and the Logic School never really leaves grammar behind, so rhetoric has been present in a gospel school student's training all along. Even kindergarteners, for example, must regularly stand before their peers—Head up! Shoulders back! Project your voice!—to practice public speaking. Rhetoric builds on the skills learned in grammar and logic, bringing them to useful fruition. It equips students not only to join but to contribute to the Great Conversation.

One of the primary ways we will love others is with our words. God loves us with his Word; husbands love their wives with their words (Eph 5:26); friends love each other by talking. Words are how we comfort, encourage, teach, correct, and express our concerns and our delights. Training in love is an education in rhetoric because love always strives to bring grace and truth into the deepest recesses of the human heart.

Rhetoric is the contemplation and communication of the true, the good, and the beautiful. Jesus is the full embodiment of truth, goodness, and beauty. He is perfect persuasion; his *ethos, pathos,* and *logos* have captured billions of hearts throughout history and continue to do so today. The drama of the cross is the majestic collision of mercy and justice, grace and truth, love and judgment—"Steadfast love and faithfulness meet; righteousness and peace kiss each other" (Ps 85:10). It is the key that perfectly fits all the locked doors of human life and nature itself. There's something so attractive about Jesus that even many who aren't Christians and don't like religion are still fascinated by him.

The gospel is also strange and mysterious. Even though Jesus is the fullness of goodness, beauty, and truth, we're told that his meekness, lowliness, and poverty made him seem ugly to us—"he had no form or majesty that we should look at him, and no beauty that we should desire him ... as one from whom men hide their faces" (Isa 53:2–3). Humanly speaking, his death was not an act of goodness but the greatest single act of injustice ever committed. The trial that led to his death wasn't full of truth but brimming with falsehoods. Yet through the ugliness, injustices, and slanders of the cross, Jesus makes our lives beautiful. His imperfection becomes our true perfection.

The deepest poetic intuition comes from the contemplation of these mysteries of gospel grace. The Rhetoric School forms students in his subtle and poetic love—in the fittingness of Jesus's words and deeds. The more our students taste the sweetness of that love, the more they will become men and women whose *ethos* is Christlike, whose *pathos* is genuine and humble, and whose *logos* is as clear, careful, and honest as glass—that they may be clear windows through whom the light of Christ can shine. "For it is you who light my lamp; the Lord my God lightens my darkness" (Ps 18:28).

8. Because Jesus is the Word of all creation, gospel math is an exploration of the orderly wisdom of Christ that has been revealed in the physical world studied by science.

As mentioned earlier, the liberal arts are divided into two parts: the Trivium and the Quadrivium. The Trivium consists of the arts of language (grammar, logic, and rhetoric). We now move to the Quadrivium (arithmetic, geometry, astronomy, and music), which mainly consists of math. Arithmetic and geometry are traditionally mathematical subjects concerning number and space, while music is math applied to sound and tempo and astronomy is math applied to space and time. In modern classical schools, the Quadrivium not only focuses on astronomy but science more broadly (earth sciences, physics, chemistry, and biology in the secondary school).

Doing math well requires a certain conscientiousness akin to the carefulness of love. Just as a gentle and faithful husband is purposeful with his words and reliable in his actions, the Lord of heaven and earth is careful and predictable in how he governs the universe. Math is the conscientious and orderly way of the Almighty with his creatures. God is not erratic but disciplined in his manner of ruling all things. The classical mind recognized a deep continuity between the moral law and the laws of nature. And Christians came to realize that the wise, predictable pattern to the universe (what the Greeks called the *logos*) is, in fact, the mind of Christ. When we study math, we glimpse God's wise ordering of the world through his Son.

Most ancient cultures believed matter to be chaotic rather than ruled by the rational, purposeful mind of a Creator. The Greeks believed in the logos, the orderly structure behind the physical universe. But it was Christians whose gospel said, "[The Logos] became flesh and dwelt among us, and we have seen his glory, glory as of the only Son from the Father, full of grace and truth" (John 1:14). This idea was revolutionary. How could something so pure and unchanging as the eternal Logos become something so unpredictable, decaying, and filled with passions as flesh? The Greek mind had set spirit and matter against each other; the study of matter couldn't lead to the deep spiritual truths of the universe. But Christians (and Jewish believers before us) have always affirmed that God reliably reveals himself in and through the physical world. "The heavens declare the glory of God" (Ps 19:1). Just as the incarnation of the Son of God is the ultimate revelation of his grace and faithfulness as our Savior, the creation of God is the revelation of his wisdom and power as our Creator: "For his invisible attributes, namely, his eternal power and divine nature, have been clearly perceived, ever since the creation of the world, in the things that have been made" (Rom 1:20).

9. Because Jesus alone satisfies the deepest desire of the human heart as both Lord and Savior, gospel singing tunes the hearts and the bodies of students to long for his love and to seek his kingdom.

Singing ties together many of the themes we've covered in this book. Throughout primary and secondary education, students sing about God's covenant promises and his grace. Singing is the backbone of the liturgy of the day. Nothing strengthens a Grammar student's memory like singing. Nothing ties together the beauty, goodness, and truth of the gospel like a beautiful song coming from the heart of one of God's children. Gospel education is filled with song.

The argument of this book has been that the goal of education is the formation of a child in love through the gospel. Throughout history, Christians have seen the liberal arts and classical learning as the most powerful vehicle and the most suitable method for just this kind of love-forming, gospel-centered education. The background sounds of a gospel school are children singing and chanting. In the Grammar School, they'll sing the memory of the human race into their minds. In the Logic and Rhetoric Schools, they will sing the beauty and subtlety of divine and human truth into their souls. In fact, the Bible tells us that singing and learning are closely tied together: "Let the word of Christ dwell in you richly, teaching and admonishing one another in all wisdom, singing psalms and hymns and spiritual songs, with thankfulness in your hearts to God" (Col 3:16).

So many Christians today fail to appreciate that learning to sing is one of the most essential skills for being a disciple of Jesus. Many Christians don't even sing in church and assume that this is no big deal because they don't know how to do it. We think what matters is what is in our hearts, and so it doesn't really matter how that is expressed with our bodies. But how can you live a life of praise to God if you don't know how to sing, or you aren't confident enough to open your mouth in worship? "Let everything that has breath praise the LORD!" (Ps 150:6). An education that forms children in love will have singing not on the margins but in the center. The music teacher must be one who inspires the culture of the school around song.

The human body is the greatest instrument in the world. When it is tuned and played rightly, nothing can touch the heart or transcend the soul like it. Not only are its tones rich and subtle, but the rational mind can join words and stories to sounds, rhythms, and melodies that resonate with the emotions. All children were gifted one of these instruments by God, and he intends for them to use it, so that all their days they will be able to sing of the wondrous love of their true, good, and beautiful Savior, Jesus Christ.

As Jesus assured his disciples, "Fear not, little flock, it is the Father's good pleasure to give you the kingdom" (Luke 12:32). This great civilization—this culture—that we have just touched on in this book is ultimately a gift of the Father's grace. "[Abraham] was looking forward to the city that has foundations, whose designer and builder is God. ... Therefore, God is not ashamed to be called their God, for he has prepared for them a city" (Heb 11:10, 16). Jesus too taught us to deeply long for this city, in his central prayer "your kingdom come, your will be done on earth as it is in heaven" (Matt 6:10). May we pray more and more for God's children to grow up surrounded by this wonderful Christian culture. May gospel education stir our little ones to love the Savior and all the rich cultural fruit he's brought to our world throughout the ages.

APPENDIX A

WHAT IS THE GOSPEL?

IN THE PROCESS of writing this book, I was asked by several readers, "What definition of the gospel are you using?" I thought I'd give a brief answer to that here. The easiest answer is that the gospel is the person of Jesus Christ. But more expansively, one of the most historic and concise summaries of the gospel is the Apostles' Creed. In the creed, there are three ways the gospel is summarized. Each of these are ways the Bible itself uses the word "gospel," and each of these aspects of the gospel is utilized in this book.

THE GOSPEL IS THE ANNOUNCEMENT THAT JESUS IS THE TRUE KING OF THE WORLD.

In the ancient world, gospel (*euangelion*) was a word often used after a military victory to announce to the people the "good news" that the king had won a decisive battle, and his kingdom was now secure. Hence, the gospel is an announcement about a king or kingdom. This is the gospel preached by Jesus himself in Mark 1:14–15: "Jesus came into Galilee, proclaiming the gospel of God, and saying, 'The time is fulfilled, and the kingdom of God is at hand; repent and believe in the gospel.'" What he means here is, the reason the kingdom has arrived is because the King has arrived.

In the creed, it says, "I believe in Jesus Christ, God's only Son, our Lord." The title "Christ" means the "Anointed One," or "Anointed King," to whom God has given the nations as his inheritance (Ps 2:7–9). Hence, the gospel is the announcement of Jesus as the true King of the world.

THE GOSPEL IS THE HISTORICAL EVENTS SURROUNDING THE PERSON OF JESUS.

In the creed, this is summarized as "Jesus ... who was conceived by the Holy Spirit, born of the Virgin Mary, suffered under Pontius Pilate, was crucified, dead, and buried. He descended into the grave, the third day he rose again from the dead, he ascended into heaven, and sits at the right hand of God the Father, from there he shall come to judge the living and the dead." These historical events—incarnation, cross, resurrection, ascension, and second coming—make up the gospel.

The apostle Paul speaks of the gospel this way in 1 Corinthians 15:1–5: "Now I would remind you, brothers, of the gospel I preached to you, which you received, in which you stand, and by which you are being saved, if you hold fast to the word I preached to you—unless you believed in vain. For I delivered to you as of first importance what I also received: that Christ died for our sins in accordance with the Scriptures, that he was buried, that he was raised on the third day in accordance with the Scriptures, and that he appeared to Cephas, then to the twelve."

Also, it should be noted that Paul considered the second coming as part of his gospel in Romans 2:16: "... on that day when, according to my gospel, God judges the secrets of men by Christ Jesus."

THE GOSPEL IS AN OFFER OF GRACE THROUGH JESUS.

In Acts 20:24, Paul refers to his message as "the gospel of the grace of God." In the creed, the grace offered in Jesus is summarized with the words: "I believe in the Holy Spirit, the holy catholic church, the communion of saints, the forgiveness of sins, the resurrection of the body, and the life everlasting."

In Reformed theology, these gifts of grace are called the "benefits of Christ's mediation" (Westminster Larger Catecheism 154), and the theological terms for them (respectively) are sanctification, adoption, justification, and glorification. Each of these saving graces is offered to sinners as a free gift, not of our own works but based on the work of Christ to be received by faith. This is why the terms "gospel-centered" and "grace-centered" are often interchangeable.

So, the gospel is best summarized in the person of Jesus—who is the true King of the world, who has worked salvation for us in history, and who offers us his saving grace as a free gift to be received by faith.

APPENDIX B

WHY CHURCH SCHOOLS?

THE TYPE OF EDUCATION described in this book, I believe, is best administered in the context of a local church and under the oversight of a local session of elders. Though education is a huge part of the church's heritage, many churches have neglected this kind of ministry. It may be that church schools can often be divisive. It may be that church leaders have not come to appreciate how essential education is to the church's mission. But the challenges and risks are without doubt worth the rewards.

Here are five reasons I believe churches need to seriously consider starting schools.

SCHOOLS ARE NEAR THE HEART OF THE MISSION OF THE CHURCH.

The mission Jesus gave to his disciples was to baptize and teach (Matt 28:18–20). Teaching has always been at the heart of Christianity. This teaching should involve biblical literacy, doctrine, and guidance in Christian living. But once we realize that all things hold together in Jesus, the areas of teaching that fall under his lordship (and therefore the purview of the church) include everything. It is appropriate for churches to take on the task of educating Christian children. Furthermore, the pattern of child discipleship should be to baptize the kids, then teach them. Education should flow naturally out of the worship service—out of the ministry of Word and sacrament on Sunday mornings.

Although the Bible ultimately entrusts the education of children to parents (Eph 6:4), our experience is that homeschooling is largely effective for parents with teaching gifts. It does not seem that, historically, the church (or synagogues before the age of the church) have found that homeschooling is a program that is effective on a large scale for God's children. To those who do it well, we strongly commend them—several of our school's most effective teachers were once homeschoolers. But generally, parents need help. This is a huge opportunity for churches to serve not only the families in their church but the broader community as well. In fact, we have found that the school has brought many families to our church and introduced them to our community.

SCHOOLS NEED THE THEOLOGICAL OVERSIGHT OF LOCAL ELDERS.

One of the biggest struggles of Christian schools is maintaining doctrinal integrity and depth. Often, a parent-led school draws families from a variety of church traditions. In an attempt to accommodate this diversity, the school ends up adopting a lowest-common-denominator Christianity or evangelicalism. The result is that the doctrinal formation of the students tends to be scattered, and each teacher teaches what is right in his or her own eyes. An evangelical school might say something like, "We are all about Jesus." What they don't realize is that when you explore the depths of who Jesus is and what he is doing in the world, it leads you into all the doctrinal questions that have divided the church. Though a classical school should welcome discussion and debate about the diversity of doctrines among denominations, at the end of the day, the school needs to land somewhere in its own beliefs.

C. S. Lewis wrote a paper in 1946 called "On the Transmission of Christianity," in which he argues that the reason most young people reject Christianity is simply because they have not been taught it well. By having a school under the oversight of a local session of elders, it frees the school to tell parents (for example), "We are a Presbyterian school. We believe that even if you come from a different tradition, the children are best served to go deeply into one tradition, instead of having a shallow version of Christianity that tries to accommodate everyone. So, you should know that your children will be catechized (i.e., indoctrinated) in the Reformed theology of the Westminster Confession and Catechisms." Our experience is that many families, even if they are not Presbyterian, appreciate this approach.

Also, in our school, we have teachers from other traditions—for example, Reformed Baptist. They have to agree to teach in accordance with our standards, but we are still able to utilize their teaching gifts. We have found this structure to be very effective.

It is crucial that there is a symbiotic relationship between the head of school and the pastor and the elders. They must all be on the same page, with a shared vision, or the church/school relationship can break down. This book is one way that we are trying to encourage that shared vision.

SCHOOLS NEED FACILITIES, AND CHURCH BUILDINGS ARE OFTEN EMPTY ALL WEEK.

One of the biggest challenges to starting new schools is facilities. Many churches are filled with classrooms that sit empty all week. Does it not inspire us to imagine the walls of our churches filled all week with young souls being discipled to offer their lives in service to Christ? Let's fill those churches with schools!

SCHOOLS BRING IN TUITION, WHICH ALLOWS CHURCHES TO EXPAND THEIR STAFF OF FULL-TIME DISCIPLE-MAKERS.

Often, the ministry of a local church is limited by the amount of tithes and offerings given by the congregation. There are only so many church staff the church can hire. But since parents pay tuition for a school, these extra funds for a church multiply the number of people involved in full-time discipleship. Currently, we have eight staff for our church but fifteen staff for our school. Having a school has tripled the number of people we have employed in full-time Christian ministry.

SCHOOLS HISTORICALLY HAVE BEEN CONNECTED TO THE MISSION AND LIFE OF THE CHURCH.

Lastly, this is our inheritance. The modern pattern of mass education was birthed in the body of Christ. Monastic schools in the early medieval era led to cathedral schools and universities in the premodern centuries. In the time of the Reformation, Protestants wanted common people to be able to read God's Word for themselves. The result was a massive expansion of education and literacy that deeply shaped the modern Western world. Still, in our day, missionaries around the world are starting schools to bring God's Word and literacy to every tribe, nation, and tongue.

Education is a Christian heritage, a gift to the world from Jesus through his church. Starting a school is immensely challenging work. But there are huge shifts happening in the world of education in our day, and churches are missing a tremendous opportunity if they don't enter this crucial work.

ENDNOTES

INTRODUCTION

1. Robert Louis Wilken, "The Church as Culture," First Things, April 1, 2004, https://www.firstthings.com/article/ 2004/04/the-church-as-culture.
2. Philip Jenkins, *The Next Christendom: The Coming of Global Christianity* (Oxford University Press, 2007), 2.
3. Aaron Earls, "Most Teenagers Drop Out of Church When They Become Young Adults," Lifeway Research, January 15, 2019, https://research.lifeway.com/2019/01/15/most-teenagers-drop-out-of-church-as-young-adults/.

CHAPTER 1: THE COVENANT CHILD

1. Douglas Wilson, *The Paideia of God and Other Essays on Education* (Canon Press, 1999), 9–15, and Werner Jaeger, *Paideia: The Ideals of Greek Culture; Volume 1, Archaic Greece, The Mind of Athens*, 2nd ed. (Oxford University Press, 1973), xxiii–xxiv.

CHAPTER 2: A GOSPEL CULTURE

1. G. K. Chesterton, *Heretics/Orthodoxy* (Thomas Nelson, 2000), 209.
2. The first of Luther's Ninety-Five Theses reads: "When our Lord and Master Jesus Christ said, 'Repent' (Matt. 4:17), he willed the entire life of believers to be one of repentance." This theme is present throughout Luther's works. Take, for example, his reflections on the implications of baptism in the

Small Catechism ("The Sacrament of Baptism," Concordia Publishing House, 2019, https://catechism.cph.org/en/sacrament-of-holy-baptism.html): "The Old Adam in us should by daily contrition and repentance be drowned and die with all sins and evil desires, and that a new man should daily emerge and arise to live before God in righteousness and purity forever." Thanks to Josh Pauling for this quotation.

3. Dallas Willard, *Renovation of the Heart: Putting on the Character of Christ* (NavPress, 2022), 192.
4. John R. W. Stott, *The Cross of Christ*, 20th Anniversary Edition (IVP Books, 2006), 290.
5. William Langland, "Vision One, Prologue," in *Piers Plowman*, Reissue Edition (Oxford University Press, 2009), 5.
6. G. K. Chesterton, *Saint Thomas Aquinas & Saint Francis of Assisi* (Ignatius Press, 2002), 267.
7. C. S. Lewis, *Present Concerns* (Harcourt, 1986), 15.

CHAPTER 3: THE LITURGY OF THE DAY

1. James K. A. Smith, *You Are What You Love: The Spiritual Power of Habit* (Brazos, 2016), 21.
2. "For Calvin, monastics are mistaken only insofar as they make elite, difficult, and rare what should be ordinary, accessible, and common in Christian communities: namely, whole human lives formed in and through the church's distinctive repertoire of disciplines, from singing psalms to daily prayer to communing with Christ at the sacred supper" (Matthew Myer Boulton, *Life in God: John Calvin, Practical Formation and the Future of Protestant Theology* [Eerdmans, 2011], 15, quoted by "Calvin's Geneva as Catechetical Polis," *Catechesis Institute*, April 9, 2018, https://www.catechesisrenewal.com/blog/2018/04/09-geneva-as-catechetical-polis).
3. Dietrich Bonhoeffer and Walter Brueggemann, *Psalms: The Prayer Book of the Bible* (Broadleaf Books, 2022), 26.
4. Peter J. Leithart, *The Four: A Survey of the Gospels* (Canon Press, 2010), 121–28.
5. Dietrich Bonhoeffer, *Life Together* (HarperOne, 1954), 66.
6. Robert Littlejohn and Charles Evans, *Wisdom and Eloquence: A Christian Paradigm for Classical Learning* (Crossway, 2006), 25.
7. Eric Metaxas, *Bonhoeffer: Pastor, Martyr, Prophet, Spy* (Thomas Nelson, 2010), 270.

CHAPTER 4: A CHRISTIAN WORLDVIEW

1. C. S. Lewis, *The Weight of Glory and Other Addresses* (Touchstone Books, 1996), 106.
2. For more on this historical influence, see: Tom Holland, *Dominion: How the Christian Revolution Remade the World* (Basic Books, 2021); Larry Hurtado, *Destroyer of the Gods: Early Christian Distinctiveness in the Roman World* (Baylor University Press, 2016); Rodney Stark, *The Victory of Reason: How Christianity Led to Freedom, Capitalism, and Western Success* (Random House, 2005) and *The Triumph of Christianity: How the Jesus Movement Became the World's Largest Religion* (HarperOne, 2011); and Robert Louis Wilken, *The First Thousand Years: A Global History of Christianity* (Yale University Press, 2012).
3. For the statistics, see Gregory Smith et al., "America's Changing Religious Landscape, Chapter 1," Pew Research Center, May 12, 2015, https://www.pewresearch.org/religion/wp-content/uploads/sites/7/2015/05/RLS-08-26-full-report.pdf. For an account of American evangelicals' lack of cultural influence, see James Davison Hunter, *To Change the World: The Irony, Tragedy, and Possibility of Christianity in the Late Modern World* (Oxford University Press, 2010), 18–27, 84–92.
4. G. K. Chesterton, *What's Wrong with the World* (London: Cassell), 204–5.
5. "Nevertheless, we can be quite certain that the Reformers considered all of these essential to baptism. … When the child gets to be ten or twelve years old, the child will be expected to learn the catechism and, having learned the catechism, to make a profession of faith. When one looks at the catechism that was used, it becomes particularly clear. It is indeed an elaborate confession of faith in which the Apostles' Creed is learned, explained, and confessed" (Hughes Oliphant Old, *Worship: Reformed According to Scripture*, rev. and exp. ed. [Westminster John Knox, 2002], 13).

CHAPTER 5: TRAINING IN WISDOM

1. Cornelius Plantinga Jr., *Not the Way It's Supposed to Be: A Breviary of Sin* (Eerdmans, 1996), 115.
2. In the early chapters of the Institutes, John Calvin centers wisdom on an integrated knowledge of God, self, and world: "Again, it is certain that man never achieves a clear knowledge of himself unless he has first looked upon God's face, and then descends from contemplating him to scrutinize himself" (John Calvin, *Institutes of the Christian Religion*, I.1.2). "Lest anyone, then be excluded from access to happiness, he not only sowed in men's minds that seed of religion of which we have spoken but revealed himself

and daily discloses himself in the whole workmanship of the universe. As a consequence, men cannot open their eyes without being compelled to see him" (Calvin, *Institutes*, I.5.1).

3. In Nancy Pearcy's book *Total Truth: Liberating Christianity from Its Cultural Captivity* (Crossway, 2005), she has a chapter exploring this dualism in academia and philosophy (pp. 97–121). One example she gives of this contradiction: "To show how common this pattern is, let's consider a few more examples. Pinker's colleague at MIT, Marvin Minsky, is famous for his catchy phrase that the human mind is nothing but 'a three-pound computer made of meat.' But in his book *The Society of Mind*, he too takes a leap of faith. 'The physical world provides no room for freedom of will,' he writes. And yet, 'that concept is essential to our models of the mental realm. Too much of our psychology is based on it for us to ever give it up. [And so] we're virtually forced to maintain that belief, even though we know it's false' " (p. 109, quoting Marvin Minsky, *The Society of Mind* [Simon & Schuster, 1985], 307).
4. Alan Jacobs, *The Narnian: The Life and Imagination of C. S. Lewis* (HarperOne, 2005), 162.
5. "Even before the pandemic, anxiety and depression were becoming more common among children and adolescents, increasing 27 percent and 24 percent respectively from 2016 to 2019. By 2020, 5.6 million kids (9.2%) had been diagnosed with anxiety problems and 2.4 million (4.0%) had been diagnosed with depression" (Aubrianna Osorio, "Research Update: Children's Anxiety and Depression on the Rise," Georgetown University Health Policy Institute Center for Children and Families, March 24, 2022, https://ccf.georgetown.edu/2022/03/24/research-update-childrens-anxiety-and-depression-on-the-rise/#:~:text=Even%20before%20the%20pandemic%2C%20anxiety,had%20been%20diagnosed%20with%20depression). See also Mark Sayers, *A Non-Anxious Presence: How a Changing and Complex World Will Create a Remnant of Renewed Christian Leaders* (Moody, 2022), 39–42, and Edwin Friedman, *A Failure of Nerve: Leadership in the Age of the Quick Fix* (Church Publishing, 2017), 57–100.
6. C. H. Spurgeon, *Lectures to My Students* (Hendrickson, 2011), 151.
7. This quote came from a personal conversation with George Grant.
8. Thanks to Josh Pauling for this insight.
9. There are several great books that have given fuller treatments of the Trivium than what is found in Sayers's essay. A few recommendations: Stratford Caldecott, *Beauty in the Word: Rethinking the Foundations of Education* (Angelico Press, 2012); Robert Littlejohn and Charles T. Evans, *Wisdom and Eloquence: A Christian Paradigm for Classical Learning* (Crossway, 2006);

and Kevin Clark, DLS, and Ravi Scott Jain, *The Liberal Arts Tradition: A Philosophy of Christian Classical Education* (Classical Academic Press, 2013).

CHAPTER 6: GRAMMAR

1. By magic, I don't mean the sinister attempt at manipulation of words, objects, or people in order to control them or serve ourselves. Such practices stand in direct contradiction to God's Word. I'm referring to magic in the popular sense of something mysterious and wonderful that can't be expressed simply by appeal to technical or scientific explanations.
2. Kevin Clark, DLS, and Ravi Scott Jain, *The Liberal Arts Tradition: A Philosophy of Christian Classical Education* (Classical Academic Press, 2013), 38–39.
3. Saint Augustine, *On Christian Teaching* (Oxford University Press, 1999), 8.
4. E. D. Hirsch Jr., *Cultural Literacy: What Every American Needs to Know* (Vintage, 1988), 53.
5. Dorothy Sayers, quoted in Hirsch, *Cultural Literacy*, 30.
6. Stratford Caldecott, *Beauty in the Word: Rethinking the Foundations of Education* (Angelico Press, 2012), 48–49.
7. Classically, there are some nuances and developments in the subtle differences between "art" and "skill." Art is the intuitive grasp of an area of human pursuit. Skill is the effective ability to pursue it. For my purposes here, I will largely be using the words interchangeably.

CHAPTER 7: LOGIC

1. Huston Smith, *The World's Religions* (HarperCollins, 1991), 317.
2. Rudolf Euchen, quoted in Herman Bavinck, *Christian Worldview* (Crossway, 2019), 119: "History meant far more to Christianity than it did to the ancient world. It was the Christian conviction that the divine had appeared in the domain of time, not as a pale reflection but in the whole fullness of its glory; hence as the dominating central point of the whole it must relate the whole past to itself and unfold the whole future out of itself. The unique character of this central occurrence was beyond all doubt. Christ could not come again and yet again to be crucified; hence as the countless historical cycles of the ancient world disappeared, there was no longer the old eternal recurrence of things. History ceased to be a uniform rhythmic repetition and became a comprehensive whole, a single drama. Man was now called on to accomplish a complete transformation, and this made his life incomparably tenser than it had been in the days when man had merely to unfold an already existing nature. Hence in Christianity, and

nowhere else, lie the roots of a higher valuation of history and of temporal life in general."

Bavinck goes on: "Christianity is itself the central content of this great history. ... Everyone who thinks it through must come to this insight: apart from and without Christianity there is no possibility of history in the proper sense, no history of the world and humanity" (120).

3. Thanks to Josh Pauling for this insight. See also Philip Jenkins, *The Lost History of Christianity: The Thousand-Year Golden Age of the Church in the Middle East, Africa, and Asia—and How It Died* (HarperOne, 2008).
4. Philip Jenkins, *The Next Christendom: The Coming of Global Christianity* (Oxford University Press, 2007).
5. G. K. Chesterton, *St. Francis of Assisi* (Image Books, 1957), 25–26.
6. Richard Fletcher, *The Barbarian Conversion: From Paganism to Christianity* (University of California Press, 1999).
7. Some might wonder how much Charlemagne and Alfred's intentions were truly about power. There is no question their motivations were likely mixed. For an account of Charlemagne's spiritual vision for his empire, see Tom Holland, Dominion: *How the Christian Revolution Remade the World* (Basic Books, 2021), 201–21.
8. Holland, *Dominion*, 206.
9. One might ask about the contributions to science of both the ancient Greeks and Arabs during the Golden Age of Islam. There is no doubt that their learning was extensive and that Christians benefited mightily from their wisdom. But a parallel question is: If these cultures had such extensive histories of learning, why did science never fully blossom among them? The likely answer is that there were fatal flaws in their worldviews that inhibited their learning. Though Aristotle's approach was empirical, the Greeks saw matter as fundamentally chaotic and so failed to discover the laws of nature that matter obeyed. A similar problem existed among the Chinese. And, again, the Arabs had theological views of Allah's relationship to creation that caused them to not think of nature as predictable. The Bible's understanding of God as orderly, rational, and covenantal (meaning he submitted himself to his own law) gave a worldview that made the discovery of science possible. For more on this, see Tom Holland, *Dominion: How the Christian Revolution Remade the World* (Basic Books, 2021), 12–23.
10. G. K. Chesterton, *The Everlasting Man* (Ignatius, 1993), 250.
11. God is three and one. Jesus is man and God. Jesus became sin for us but is sinless. We are saved through faith alone, but true faith never is alone. God is sovereign over creation, yet we are still responsible. The nations of the earth will be discipled, but Christians will always be taking up their crosses and find themselves on the margins of society. Baptism saves you

(1 Pet 3:21), but not all baptized people are saved. We must be in the world but not of the world. The church is God's elect, but not all in the church are elect. The list goes on and on.

These paradoxes are also true in ethics. Love has both grace and truth, forgiveness and justice. Don't overwork; don't be lazy. Diligently discipline your children, but don't exasperate them with harshness. Basically, every ethical question has two opposite ditches that need to be avoided. See Robert S. Rayburn, *The Truth in Both Extremes: Paradox in Biblical Revelation* (Wipf & Stock, 2021), and G. K. Chesterton, *Heretics/Orthodoxy* (Thomas Nelson, 2000), 237–55.

12. "Moreover, the liberal arts and sciences have descended to us from the heathen. We are, indeed, compelled to acknowledge that we have received astronomy, and the other parts of philosophy, medicines and the order of civil government, from them. Nor is it to be doubted, that God has thus liberally enriched them with excellent favors that their impiety might have the less excuse. But, while we admire the riches of his favor which he has bestowed on them, let us still value far more highly that grace of regeneration with which he peculiarly sanctifies his elect unto himself" (John Calvin, *Calvin's Commentaries*, vol. 1 [Baker Books, 2009], 218). See also Saint Augustine, *On Christian Doctrine*, book two.
13. G. K. Chesterton, quoted in Stratford Caldecott, *Beauty in the Word: Rethinking the Foundations of Education* (Angelico Press, 2012), 68.
14. In some respects, questions about the authority of the Bible should certainly be welcomed. But we must be careful not to imply that its authority can be proven by seemingly objective evidence or methods. If you try to prove the authority of the Bible, you can only do so by looking to some alternative or additional authority (history, philosophy, archeology, church fathers). To do so is to place something other than God's own Word at the foundation of our knowledge. Our students must come to terms with the reality that God establishes his own Word's authority—since there is no authority so trustworthy as God himself.

CHAPTER 8: RHETORIC

1. C. S. Lewis, *A Preface to Paradise Lost: Being the Ballard Matthews Lectures Delivered at University College, North Wales, 1941* (Oxford University Press, 1961), 53.
2. Aristotle, *Rhetoric*, I.2.
3. Malcom Gladwell, *Outliers: The Story of Success* (Little, Brown, 2008), 47–50.

4. Saint Augustine, *The City of God* (Modern Library, 1993), 698. Maybe after seven hundred pages on theology and culture, Augustine realized he had veered too far in one direction and needed to be more active!
5. Quintilian, *Institutio Oratoria*, 12.2.4, quoted in Dave McClellan, *Preaching by Ear* (Weaver Book Company, 2014), 42.
6. Contemporary thinkers like Cal Newport have advocated this kind of contemplation and its unique value through the notion of "deep work." See his *Deep Work* (Grand Central Publishing, 2016).
7. C. S. Lewis, *The World's Last Night: And Other Essays* (Harcourt, 1987), 42.
8. See especially James S. Taylor, *Poetic Knowledge: The Recovery of Education* (State University of New York Press, 1997).
9. Flannery O'Connor, "Fiction Is a Subject with a History—It Should Be Taught That Way," in *Collected Works* (Library of America, 1988), 850–52.

CHAPTER 9: MATH AND SCIENCE

1. For examples in the writings of C. S. Lewis, see his *The Discarded Image: An Introduction to Medieval and Renaissance Literature* (Cambridge University Press, 1964), 94–95, 108–9.
2. The complicated progression of this view of the universe is carefully narrated in Charles Taylor, *A Secular Age* (The Belknap Press of Harvard University Press, 2007), especially Parts I and II. Though the "disenchantment" of the universe was deeply impacted by Calvin's vision of God's sovereign providence—which flattened the hierarchical, medieval view of the cosmos—it eventually developed into a "providential deism" over the course of the Enlightenment. It's Calvin's view of the universe under God's wise, providential care I'm endorsing here.
3. See Lewis, *Discarded Image*, 94.
4. The Greeks certainly had some insight into the rational way God ruled the world, but because of their unbelief (Rom 1:18–25), they could not construct a true and full picture. As John Frame puts it, speaking about the Greek philosopher Heraclitus: "The source of stability Heraclitus called the logos, probably the first philosophically significant use of this term. Logos has a variety of meanings: 'word,' 'reason,' 'rational account.' Heraclitus believed in a principle governing change, to keep that change within rational bounds. … We do see here another assertion of the Greek rationalism in the logos. Reason must be our guide, Heraclitus tells us, even if we don't see how it can be reliable. Rationality must exist not only in our minds, but as an aspect of the universe. But he thus invokes reason, in effect, by an act of faith. On the other hand, the changing flux amounts to irrationalism. For Heraclitus virtually concedes that reason cannot deal with reality unless it is somehow constant. But at the elemental levels, reality is anything but

constant" (John Frame, *A History of Western Philosophy and Theology* [P&R Publishing, 2015], 55–56).

5. Johannes Kepler, "Epitome astronomiae Coperinicanae," in *Gesammelte Werke* 7, 208, quoted in Max Casper, *Kepler* (Abelard-Schuman, 1959), 381.
6. Stratford Caldecott, *Beauty in the Word: Rethinking the Foundations of Education* (Angelico Press, 2012), 30.
7. See Lewis, *Discarded Image*, 16–17.
8. G. K. Chesterton, *Saint Thomas Aquinas: The Dumb Ox* (Image Books, 1956), 66.
9. Vern Poythress, quoted in John Frame, *Christianity Considered* (Lexham Press, 2018), 48.
10. Richard Dawkins, *The Blind Watchmaker: Why the Evidence of Evolution Reveals a Universe Without Design* (W. W. Norton, 1996), 10.
11. My personal view is what I call an "accelerated old earth." Since all things were made through Christ (Col 1:16), his miracles in the Gospels are a picture of his creative power as the Lord of nature. Turning water into wine is something he does every year in nature: As the rain falls, grape vines transform the water into grapes, and they are smashed and fermented. So, the miracle at Cana was a natural process done quickly through Christ. That wine was good wine, i.e., aged wine. It is the same with the creation as a whole—not made as a "trick" by God, but a long natural process was done quickly through Christ—that is, it was accelerated. I believe this view allows us to read Genesis as six twenty-four-hour days while also studying the earth scientifically as an "old" earth. I also believe this view "re-enchants" our imaginative view of the universe as the miraculous, symbolic, and beautiful craftsmanship of our Lord.
12. The beginning of history and the "last day" have in common that the Word of God (who is Jesus Christ) enters the world suddenly, first as a creative Word and in the end as a Word of judgment. Just as we cannot calculate when the judgment will arrive in the future (Matt 24:36), neither can we calculate when the beginning occurred in the past.
13. A helpful resource on this question is the position paper on creation from the Presbyterian Church in America. Our church's school has adopted the following statement:

    > We believe that the truth about God, our world, and what it means to be human is perfectly revealed to us in the inerrant word of God, the Bible. During the modern era, American educational institutions believed that free inquiry in science would lead to a knowledge of the truth, and many Christians assumed that would be the case. Over the course of the last 150 years, Scientism (the religion of science) became a primary form of spiritual rebellion against our Creator. This belief in free inquiry did not adequately recognize the effects of sin on the

scientific mind. Reason is largely used by humans to justify whatever it is they want to believe or do. Science is no exception.

All science is built on unproven assumptions about the natural world. Therefore, science and Scripture are not two alternate paths to the truth about reality. Science is a body of knowledge built on the foundational assumptions given by the Scriptures. The Bible says the world was created by a rational, covenantal, and unchanging God. It was this theological worldview that led Christians to discover the early scientific discoveries of the Enlightenment. Any attempt for science to undermine the teaching of Scripture actually undermines the very foundations on which science was built:

- All things seen and unseen were created by God out of nothing by the power of his Word.
- God's creation is very good.
- He is the Almighty Sovereign over all that happens, ruling and ordering his creation according to his wise and holy purposes.
- God created the earth in the space of six days, as recorded in Genesis 1.
- God created all animals according to their kinds.
- God created man by a unique act of creation from the dust of the earth, and the woman from the rib of the man.
- God created the man and woman after his own image.

The Westminster Confession of Faith (our doctrinal standard) says this about creation:

> It pleased God the Father, Son, and Holy Ghost, for the manifestation of the glory of His eternal power, wisdom, and goodness, in the beginning, to create or make of nothing the world, and all things therein, whether visible or invisible, in the space of six days, and all very good. (WCF 4.1)

Evolution has been the dominant theory of origin by which modern secularists have argued that the Bible is false, thus being a primary vehicle for leading our society into unbelief. Therefore, TCS takes a strong position against any form of evolution as explanatory regarding life on earth.

- Evolution is a modern origins myth that is not only hostile to the revelation of the Bible but has also been shown to be false scientifically. The fossil record uncovered over the past 150 years does

not reveal a gradual connection between species, but fossil types appear in clumps, suggesting something much closer to the Bible's teaching that God created living beings "according to their kind" (Gen. 1:21-25).
- Evolution should not be regarded as a scientific theory, as it can in no way be tested using the scientific method. There is no repeatable experiment that can verify its claims. It should be regarded as something closer to natural history.
- Evolution is not simply a natural history, but it plays a role in our culture as a story about the meaning of life, emphasizing survival of the fittest ("the strong eat the weak"). This is contrary to the Bible's vision of the Creator God being a fountain of goodness and life and the creation being a gift of divine grace. Evolution is a worldview hostile to Christianity.

We recognize that the questions about the origins of life and the age of the earth are two very different questions (though related in the minds of many). While we reject evolution as a theory, we do recognize that the earth bears the marks of being very old, which raises honest questions about how that squares with Genesis 1. As a ministry of Christ Church Bellingham, a member church of the Presbyterian Church in America (PCA), we agree with the PCA's published study committee paper on Creation that recommends a mutual respect for four different readings of Genesis 1 within the church:

- Literal six, 24-hour day creation
- Day Age theory (the six days represent long periods of time in consecutive order)
- Analogical week (Genesis 1 is making an analogy between God's work week and ours, but is not a literal description of how God formed the earth)
- Framework Hypothesis (this is a literary structure for Genesis 1 that can actually work with any of the other three views)

As Augustine wrote, "Let each one, then, take it as he pleases, for it is so profound a passage that it may well suggest, for the exercise of the reader's tact, many opinions, and none of them widely departing from the rule of faith" (Augustine, City of God, Book XI.32). The preference of CCB and TCS is the literal 24-hour creation view, as it seems to be Moses' intent in writing it (see Exodus 20:8–11). We also respect these other views, and in our science classes students will learn some of the reasons why it seems the earth bears marks of being very old.

Just as the wine that Jesus made out of water instantly would have bore the marks of aged wine, we believe it is not a contradiction to say that the earth was made in the space of six literal days less than 10,000 years ago and still bears the marks of being very old. For "with the Lord one day is as a thousand years, and a thousand years as one day" (2 Peter 3:8).

We also recognize that the Bible does not give much information about what exactly unfolded in God's creation of the earth. We are content with the limits of human knowledge, and we worship and trust God as the Lord of his creation. Ecclesiastes 3:11 tells us, "He has made everything beautiful in its time. Also, he has put eternity into man's heart, yet so that he cannot find out what God has done from the beginning to the end."

14. Augustine, *City of God*, Book XI.32.
15. Of course, scientists have observed mutations in plants and animals (they do happen), but rarely do these mutations result in biological advantages. And because of the time necessary for Darwinian evolution, contemporary scientists could never observe enough mutations to see any form of complex development.
16. Jerry A. Coyne, *Why Evolution Is True* (Penguin, 2009). Coyne has been a professor at the University of Chicago in the Department of Ecology and Evolution for the past twenty years, where he specializes in evolutionary genetics and the origin of new species.
17. Stephen Jay Gould, quoted in Stephen C. Meyer, *Darwin's Doubt: The Explosive Origin of Animal Life and the Case for Intelligent Design* (HarperOne, 2013), 15–17. Meyer points out that this same argument was made even in Darwin's day (13–14).
18. Donald E. Johnson, *Probability's Nature and Nature's Probability: A Call to Scientific Integrity* (Booksurge Publishing, 2009).
19. Thomas Nagel, *Mind & Cosmos: Why the Materialist Neo-Darwinian Conception of Nature Is Almost Certainly False* (Oxford University Press, 2012). Similar arguments are made in C. S. Lewis, *Miracles: A Preliminary Study* (HarperOne, 2015).
20. C. S. Lewis, *Christian Reflections* (Eerdmans, 1995), 87.
21. Lewis, *Christian Reflections*, 89.

CHAPTER 10: SINGING

1. Saint Augustine of Hippo, *The Confessions: Saint Augustine of Hippo*, ed. David Vincent Meconi, S. J. (Ignatius Press, 2012), 240.
2. Peter J. Leithart, *Traces of the Trinity: Signs of God in Creation and Human Experience* (Brazos Press, 2015), 86.

3. See C. S. Lewis, "Good Work and Good Works," in *The World's Last Night: And Other Essays* (Harcourt, 1987), 78–79.
4. Lewis goes on to explicitly name Christian singing ("Good Work," 80–81).

NINE THESES OF GOSPEL EDUCATION

1. Dorothy Sayers, "The Lost Tools of Learning," 12-14, https://www.pccs.org/wp-content/uploads/2016/06/LostToolsOfLearning-DorothySayers.pdf.

www.ingramcontent.com/pod-product-compliance
Lightning Source LLC
Chambersburg PA
CBHW021142090426
42740CB00008B/901

* 9 7 8 1 5 4 0 9 0 6 0 0 7 *